April 19

To Chris + M

C000156638

As you are part of
the story it is fitting,
that you get a copy.

Thanks for what you have
sown into our lives.

Trevor + Linda

Falling from grace into Grace

AND BEING CAUGHT BY THE FATHER

Falling from grace into Grace

AND BEING CAUGHT BY THE FATHER

"He will turn the hearts of the fathers to their children, and the hearts of the children to their fathers;"
Malachi 4:6

TREVOR GALPIN

©2015

Published by Fatherheart Ministries Taupo

First Published in Great Britain in 2013.

British Library Cataloguing in Publication Data
ISBN: 978-0-9575318-0-2

Cover design by Mathilde Oord

Dedicated to my wife, my dearest friend and love of my life, for her unfailing support, encouragement through life and her help in editing this book. To Linda.

Also,
Dedicated to my three wonderful children: Nick, Sanna and Chrissie for whom I wrote this book in order to help them know better the man who is their father.

CONTENTS

FOREWORD

A spiritual father of mine; Jack Winter, once said, "never follow a man who doesn't limp"! He is of course referring to how Jacob, a man who really sought God's blessing, came face to face with himself at Peniel and in deep wrestling with God came out of it with a new name and a new walk as a new day was dawning. A new day with a new grace.

The apostle Paul stated that in him there dwelt no good thing. He was a man who came face to face also with his real self and found grace. The great apostle Peter also on two occasions was faced up with what was really in his heart. Once by Jesus when he had deluded himself that his human zeal was a godly thing. Then secondly when Paul faced him up with his prejudices against non-Jews and his fear of the Jewish leaders. King David was a man whom God himself chose to be king because he saw that he was a man "after God's own heart". Yet as a mature and greatly significant man in God's work he sinned. The interesting thing is that God purposely, when there was a great opportunity to remove him from his Kingship, reinstated him and blessed him as King till his dying day.

I have discovered that if anyone appears to have no faults that is exactly what it is - an appearance. Many leaders walk the tightrope of keeping up an appearance of faultlessness. Some seminaries teach their future pastors never to make friends of those in their churches being given this as the reason. "If they see your faults they will realise that you are just as human as them and you will lose your authority in their eyes."

The reality is we are all on a path to perfection. None have reached it except the one we are learning to walk like. The One whose humanity was finally made perfect as he died on the Cross. Jesus, our older brother, the firstborn of many brethren, is our model, goal and guide. We are on our way to be conformed into His likeness.

In this book Trevor has been extremely transparent in his pathway in this life we call Christianity. He has faced himself. He lost everything including reputation, the most freeing thing to lose. He lost all security and many of his friends, if those ones were really friends. He lost himself and his calling and destiny in ministry. So bravely Linda stuck with him as they struggled together through some dark years.

But God is a God of patience and compassion. Like a mother with her young He comforts. Like a mother hen with her chicks He hides them under His wing. Like a strong tower he supplies a place to run to.

God is a God of redemption! As He did with Moses, with David, with Samson, with Judah, with Naomi, with Peter, with Paul and with so many saints throughout the ages there is a new day for each. Beware the God who forgives sin and restores His loved ones. Reject the loved and you reject the Lover.

It is a great source of satisfaction and joy to Denise and me to have been able to play a part in the redemption and restoration God has done in Trevor and Linda's lives. God's calling and gifting are never taken away by Him!

It is amazing to watch as Trevor and Linda are going from strength to strength as they walk deeper and deeper into the Father's love for them. As they realise Father's love being poured into them more and more that love is also pouring out to the nations of the earth. Thousands of people are being affected by their lives - more than in the former years! (But then the latter house is always greater than the former.) As Trevor and Linda walk alongside us in the Fatherheart

Ministries international team we are very proud of them. They hold a senior place in our ministry which is all made up of candidates for the Cave of Adullam. They travel all over the globe eleven months of the year fulfilling prophecies given decades ago in the early part of their walks with God. I highly recommend them to you and know many will find great encouragement from this book.

James Jordan - Founder and Director of Fatherheart Ministries, author of "Sonship".

~

PREFACE

I started to write this book fifteen years ago. At least I started to think about writing it fifteen years ago. It was at a time when I was in the midst of great sadness when I had really no idea what was going on in my life. I was struggling with what I perceived to be a great sense of injustice. I am so glad I did not get very far with writing it as I was full of pain and I had not even begun to see what God the Father was doing in my life. This book has now become about the journey that God my Father has me on which began many years before the time of sadness. It is a lot about what I did not know and how I came to know I did not know! It is also about the journey of how he revealed himself to me. Before it would have been a blessing to no one. Now my hearts desire is that it will be a blessing to those who read it and maybe help some to find him as a real Father to them too.

I did not intend to write an autobiography as that feels somewhat self indulgent and is really the preserve of the famous. However, there is a great deal about me in the book which I am a little embarrassed about. I had not originally intended to do that, but as it has unfolded, to make any sense of my journey there was a need for quite a large amount of personal detail. I have not included everything because that would be unnecessary and somewhat boring. Also it tends to focus on the failures and weaknesses rather than the triumphs and strengths, but that is because I have realised that in my weakness I have seen the greatest examples of the incredible love that the Father has lavished on me throughout my life. In the end, this book is about the patience of God as he has waited for me, loved me and cared for me throughout my life. The first letter of Paul to the Corinthians

Chapter 13 verse 4 says, '*Love is patient and love is kind*'. This book is probably more about that than anything else.

I have had a great interest in Church History since my days at Theological College and I love to see the way threads are tied together in an historical way. There is an aspect of this book that reflects the history of the church, especially in Britain during the last sixty years. It has been an amazing privilege to have seen and been part of what God has done in the world throughout these years and to have been involved in some of it in a very personal way. So I have tried to add as much detail to these moves of God as possible in order to provide some context not only for my own life but for many of us caught up in the drama and excitement of these movements and events. However it is not an objective history rather it reflects my experience and perspective of the events described.

Finally, I have written this book because a fair amount of my story comes out in the course of speaking at Fatherheart Ministries Schools and Conferences on which I teach these days. This tends to be in a somewhat random way. So I thought I would put it down on paper in a sequential and chronological way. My aim has been to present the wonderful, patient and compelling love of God my Father and to encourage anyone who reads it to allow him to reveal that love to them also. There is little else I want to do with my life now than proclaim this love and celebrate with him in the joy that he has in his heart over each one of us who comes home. As you will read in this book I have discovered that the good news is about a Father who wants his sons and daughters to come home.

I'd like to add one last thing and that is to thank those who have helped me on my journey home to my Father. Many of them are mentioned in this book and you will read about them in its pages.

Some have not been mentioned specifically but have been there through much of the journey. I'm not going to turn this into one of those acceptance speeches at the Oscars where winners mention everyone they can think of because they always leave someone out. Instead I am going to mention just one person who has been alongside me on this journey and that is my wife Linda. She has experienced the vast majority of this book as we have known each other since we were sixteen years old. She has been with me in the pain and trauma and has experienced so much of it herself. She stood beside me in my darkest moments and has also shared our greatest joys and triumphs. It is Linda who deserves an Oscar! I literally would not be where I am today had she not hung in there with me and at times held me up.

I am so thankful that the Father has provided such a wonderful helper and partner for me. Linda has been alongside me in almost every page of this book, faithfully never giving up on me and long sufferingly listening to my ramblings. She is my love and my delight and I have been so greatly blessed that she continues to be alongside me today on the journey. In many ways this is our journey rather than my journey. So thank you Linda.

~

INTRODUCTION

One evening in early March 1996, my life as I had known it came to an abrupt end and my life as I now know it began. At the time I had no idea that this day would become in every way the pivotal day of my life.

I stood before a group of nearly two hundred people whom I had loved and cared for as their Pastor for over seven years. Many of them had become Christians during those years. I had baptised them and nurtured them. I had taught them all I knew about God to the very best of my ability. For many of them I had conducted their weddings, welcomed their new born children into the family of the church and buried their relatives. I had laughed with them, cried with them, partied with them, dined with them, served them and loved them.

In the front row were Linda and our three children. As I looked at my family their faces all showed the strain of the previous days. They had only known for a few weeks what I was about to say to the assembled church. They were still reeling from the shock that their father and husband was not the man that they had thought he was.

Alongside them were a group of my friends, all of them my fellow leaders and elders in the church and from the network of churches of which we were part. Their faces were serious and fixed on me. They knew what I was about to say. They had agreed the draft of the statement I was about to deliver. They were disappointed and sad. They were angry and shocked. They felt I had let them down, let the church down, let my family down and let myself down. Most of all it had been made very clear to me that they felt I had let the Lord down. Several had tears in their eyes.

I stood before them all. I looked across the congregation and could feel the sense of tension that was spreading across the room. I could see bewilderment on some people's faces and anxiety in some people's eyes. After a brief pause I drew a deep breath and began to speak and read my prepared statement. I told them about my life and how I had let everyone down by having "a moral failure" some years before, that was the agreed terminology. How I had sinned. How I had hidden it. How I had cried out to God for forgiveness. How I had decided in recent weeks to begin to address the underlying issues. I told them it had been decided that, as a consequence, I needed to resign my position as the leading elder of the church.

In that moment everything in my life changed. The following few years were without a doubt the hardest and most painful years of my life, not just for me but for Linda and the family also.

When Linda and I look back on those years today, we think that they were certainly the most difficult years of our lives and that we would not want to go through them ever again. However we also agree we would not trade them for anything. That day we started out on a journey that would lead us home to God our Father and to discover his unconditional love and favour for us. For me, it was a falling from grace into grace, his grace, his love and his comforting arms. This book is that story.

~

CHAPTER ONE

It's Another Boy

~

"It's another boy!" There was a note of disappointment in the voice of my father when he announced my birth to the wider family. My parents had reached their forties and another child was desperately wanted. They had been especially entertaining the thought of a girl to complete their little family. The aged aunts, my father's five older sisters, had all been knitting furiously in preparation and they were knitting pink booties and cardigans. The first child, my older brother, had been born some years earlier. He was a very bright and intelligent boy who clearly was going to excel in any discipline that involved numbers. His future successful career as a mathematician reflects this early ability and interest. He apparently could add up the house numbers along the street as he was taken out for a stroll in his push chair. Endless family tales of his brilliance and outstanding good behaviour were circulated. I cannot begin to imagine the internal pressure that this expectation must have produced within him. I have always had a great respect and love for him.

Unfortunately another boy was not the plan. My parents

desperately wanted a daughter. Some years later one of the aunts told me that my father was very disappointed when I was born because he so much wanted a daughter. I was to have been Brenda Mary! Very 1950s! This aunt went on to say however that she was so glad it was me that came. She was one of those people that everybody needs somewhere in their family. Someone who just pours out unconditional love into our hearts. This is what she did to both my brother and me from our earliest days. This was my auntie Mabel. She never married, but until the day she died, at age 86, she loved her boys, as she called us.

Whether there was disappointment at my arrival or not, somehow deep within my heart a seed was sown that would take root within me. I know now that the devil is the enemy of our souls and that he is a liar and murderer. This is how Jesus describes him in John's gospel chapter 8 verse 44. He continually lies to us, it is his native language, especially when we are young and vulnerable. He lied to me. He whispered in my heart that I was a disappointment and that I would always disappoint people. He lied to me about God. He told me that God was disappointed with me too and that whatever I did would never be good enough, sooner or later I would fail and then I would disappoint everyone.

Once the devil has lied to us, the lie takes root and begins to grow into a belief. At some level we begin to believe that the lie is not a lie at all but it is, in reality, the truth. As this belief grows it gives rise to a continual pattern of behaviour and thought that begins to shape our psyche, our emotional responses and our view of the world. When life's events unfold and things happen to us all these things combine to reinforce our beliefs and values. They are like branches of a tree whose trunk is our belief system and whose roots are drawing their life force and energy from the deeply imbedded lie. Our behaviours and our responses to these life events are the fruit that periodically appears. Christian people can spend hours worrying and fretting over the appearance of this fruit. They go to counsellors, pastors and therapists to receive ministry, prayer and healing. This has the effect of stripping the branch of fruit which makes them feel better, by getting cleaned up and made whole. Vows and inner promises are made that this will never happen again. Then after a while they discover that when the next major crisis or painful life event lands, the same fruit reappears. Discouragement and failure are added to the collection of fruit and the cycle begins again. All manner of false comforts are employed to manage the pain of disappointment and failure. Self medication gives rise very often to addictive patterns of behaviour. These can be alcohol, prescription drugs, smoking, illicit drugs, shopping, gambling, masturbation, pornography, workaholism, the list is huge. The variety of comforts employed to deaden the pain of our deep wounds are endless. It would take me the next forty-five years to discover this and to root out the lie. Then to know the truth that I was not a failure and a disappointment nor destined to continually repeat the cycle of trying to deal with the pain.

My parents had moved out of London to Southend in Essex after the second world war, like so many, to start a new life in the fresh air of a seaside town. Once they had moved they joined a local Baptist church within walking distance from their home. They had been part of a large Baptist Church in South London so this was an obvious decision. Church life in Great Britain in the 1950s, particularly Baptist Church life, was very different from church life of the twenty-first century.

My Father had served in the army throughout the war having married my mother in 1941. He was an accountant and therefore had been drafted into the Army Pay Corp. He attained the lofty heights of becoming an Orderly Room Sergeant. As he was posted from one provincial town to another across the country my mother went with him. Wherever they went they joined in the life of a local Baptist church. The Baptist Church in South London where they had been members had a style, typical of so many churches in the early years of the twentieth century, it was a preaching centre. The central focus and activity of the church's corporate life was the Sunday morning and evening service which culminated in a sermon. Consequently the Minister was always held in high esteem and was considered to be "good" if his sermons were biblical, occasionally mildly amusing and not too long (no more than half an hour).

Churches in the UK played a major role in many people's lives especially in the inter war years, though congregations were far smaller than they had been before the Great War. The general disillusionment in organised religion following the trauma of the first war was felt deeply in Britain. Those who remained in a church remembered nostalgically the golden era of the Victorian church when congregations were large and church attendance was a normal part of life. Names of preachers and church leaders from the past still featured in people's memories and conversations. Famous preachers of bygone years were fondly remembered and their collected sermons were the most common Christian books available. The proliferation of Christian books that is common today was only just beginning to happen in the 1950s.

One such famous preacher from the nineteenth century was C.H.Spurgeon who was remembered by many in Baptist circles and revered for his thoroughly biblical and lively preaching. Copies of some of his sermons, published all through his ministry at the Metropolitan Tabernacle at the Elephant and Castle in South London, found their way into my parents' home and sat on a shelf in a book case in the front room of our home. These were printer's galley proofs that somehow my father had come by rather than a book of collected sermons. Occasionally they were brought out on a Sunday afternoon and perused by my father, who often dozed off while flicking through them.

There was a rhythm to church and family life between the wars that my parents carried with them into their expression of religion and home life in the fifties. Reflecting on those days I can see that there was a Victorian or Edwardian feel to my parental home. The rhythm revolved around Church on Sunday and various other activities including a midweek prayer meeting, attendance at which was the bench mark of real commitment. Sundays were called 'the Lord's Day.' The front room of the family home was referred to as the Sunday Room, because it was used only on Sundays and special occasions such as Christmas. Sabbath day observance was a feature of particularly my mother's upbringing and like so many of that time was part of the rhythm to family life in the post war years. This was interpreted in a particular way. A number of fairly harmless and trivial things that were perfectly acceptable and ordinary became unwholesome on the stroke of midnight on Saturday night. Reading matter had to be wholesome on Sundays and the book case in the Sunday room was stuffed full of suitable wholesome literature. Missionary stories, books of sermons and commentaries formed the bulk of Sunday reading material. Certainly no comics or dreadful Sunday papers. One aunt who regularly visited insisted on buying 'The News Of The World' on Sundays in order to "do the fashions", a 1950s sort of lottery competition. How she endured the disapproval that would have been heaped on her amazes me. We had a television by the late fifties but programmes aired on Sundays were declared unwholesome and we were not allowed to watch them. This ban was mysteriously lifted in the early sixties when a serial called Dr. Finlay's Casebook was moved from Saturday to Sundays. From then on wholesome TV programmes could be viewed. The word wholesome still makes me shudder to this day!

Grandparents did not figure much in the family as three of them had died of various ailments and old age during the war years. Both sides of the family had their roots in some sort of Christian tradition. My mother's father had remarried a year or two after the death of my grandmother from cancer in 1942. This was always an issue of resentment for my mother who did not wholly approve of her father's new wife, especially as she had been on the periphery of the family for some years prior to her mother's death. Both her parents had been what my mother called, 'proper Christians'. They were faithful and active members of their local Baptist church and encouraged their three children to follow in their footsteps. My grandfather was a strong believer in abstinence from drinking alcohol. He was a temperance preacher, preaching regularly on the corner of Peckham Rye Park near their home in South London. He was also a pacifist and taught his children to hate violence and war. Both his sons were conscientious objectors in the Second World War and were subject to all manner of hardship as a result.

He was a strict Victorian disciplinarian and raised his children in this way. When my mother had her hair bobbed which meant she had her hair cut short in the fashion of the 1920s, my grandfather did not speak to her for a week. She was in very serious trouble when one of her aunts, who had been a music hall singer, persuaded her to go with her to a dance hall one night. She was in grave trouble on her return home late at night to find her father waiting for her to reprimand her and berate her for her blatant worldliness.

My mother and her brothers joined 'The Band of Hope', a children's and young person's organisation that promoted temperance and total abstinence from drinking alcohol. These organisations and beliefs were deeply entrenched in free churches in Britain in the first half of the twentieth century. Their roots go back to the revivals of the nineteenth century as Christians sought to address the social evils associated with drunkenness and over indulgence. The Salvation Army founded by William Booth had played a significant part in spreading this belief amongst many Christians. My mother's family were in that tradition. They had all signed the Pledge, which was a document describing their lifelong commitment to abstain from drinking alcohol. My mother to her dying day had willingly embraced this. What she was not aware of was that both my brother and I had a phase in the 1970s of making home made wine. This was usually parsnip wine, or elderberry or some such brew that was often quite potent. She assumed this was in the same class of beverage as Ginger Wine, which was a non alcoholic cordial that appeared in our childhood home each Christmas. When she visited us some years later she really enjoyed a glass of rose-hip and blackberry wine. We never did tell her! This abstinence was a feature of life that survived in our home and alcoholic beverages were never brought into the home. It was referred to as 'demon drink'. Drinking, pubs and those who frequented them were viewed with the greatest disapproval. It always amused me that there was a bottle of brandy kept in the larder with a hand written label stuck over it, 'For Medicinal Purposes Only' but I don't ever recall it being administered in such a way. I often wondered why they never appeared to notice that the level of the liquor in the bottle gradually dropped when I was in my early teens. I guess they thought it had just evaporated over time.

In the book case in our front room was a book called the Temperance Reciter. It had been published in the late nineteenth century. It came out regularly on Sunday afternoons as the book constituted wholesome reading material as opposed to comics or some such other fripperies that my father always berated me for reading on the Lord's day. I was fascinated by the book. It was aimed at children and was a compilation of rewritten nursery rhymes and poems all designed to encourage abstinence from alcohol. One that vividly sticks in my mind is a version of Alfred, Lord Tennyson's famous poem, 'The Charge of the Light Brigade', which immortalized and glorified the famous military blunder of the six hundred Light Cavalry Brigade who were massacred in an ill-fated charge into a Turkish cannonade during the Crimean War. The whole poem was rewritten and described a group of the famous six hundred charging into a public house!

> *Half a pint, half a pint, half a pint onwards,*
> *Into the public house rolled the six hundred.*
> *Forward the drink brigade charge for the beer he said;*
> *Into the valley of death rolled the six hundred....*
> *Barrels to the right of them, barrels to the left of them,*
> *Barrels in front of them, onward they blundered,*
> *Under beer's fatal spell not one man looking well,*
> *Into the public house, into the mouth of hell,*
> *Rolled the six hundred."*

It was brilliant stuff and very, very funny which made for many a happy hour on a typically rather dull and tedious Sunday afternoon.

My mother's mother, who had died in 1942, was revered as almost a family saint. She had been the pillar of respectability and a faithful and regular member of the local Baptist Church. She seemed to have had a real and vibrant Christian faith. She was greatly loved by my mother. She was described in glowing terms, especially when it came to handling her husband, my grandfather. I was always left with the feeling that for some reason my grandfather was disapproved of by my mother and that her mother was as a consequence a suffering saint. This was an identity that she herself took on in later years as a way of handling my own father's behaviour.

My father was the youngest of twelve having been born in 1915. He had an older brother, twenty-five years his senior and in between there were five surviving sisters, none of whom had married until later in life, long after the death of their parents. My paternal grandfather was born in 1866 and my grandmother in 1868. There was a huge gulf between their world and mine.

There was talk from my aunts and my father about their childhood home, a tiny brick built terrace in a Victorian suburb of South London. It had gas lighting which was finally replaced by electricity in the 1960s. There was an outside privy in the back yard and a single cold water tap in the kitchen. In this cramped environment they all lived until eventually, one by one, the sisters moved out to go into some form of domestic service. This was the way many young women found employment between the wars. My father left school at age fifteen and began to train to be an accountant attending night school and studying in the evening by candle light in his tiny bedroom. He was pushed to work in order to better himself and he constantly compared himself with those who had attained what he longed for. The aunts all talked fondly of their mother who had migrated from The Netherlands with her family in the 1860s. They too all felt that she had suffered much in her life at the hands of their father.

Their comments about their father were far more ambivalent. He was a carpenter by trade as his father and grandfather had been before him. They all said he was a heavy drinker which resulted in violence and physical abuse of his wife and daughters on a regular basis within the home. They spoke of chairs being thrown and windows broken. This behaviour was attributed to, not only drink, but various things such as a new moon or a thunderstorm! There was also whispered talk of much darker deeds that occurred behind the closed door of their parents' bedroom and even occasionally spilled out into the presence of the terrified daughters. They feared him and their fear became a factor in all of their lives. To some degree there was almost a deep seated fear of men among the sisters. None married young enough to have families of their own. At some point my grandfather became a Christian and the family attended a Plymouth Brethren assembly as a result. After my parents met my father joined my mother in the Baptist church in Peckham. However he always had an affinity with the Brethren whom he seemed to view as a Christian version of Freemasons especially as many were involved in banking and business. He looked up to them, envied them and often compared himself to them but seemed to never feel he quite belonged.

My father had great difficulty sustaining relationships with men, work colleagues and especially church leaders who were predominantly male. My parents both had many friends but all through my growing up years from time to time one or other of these people came in for my father's verbal and emotional abuse. There would be loud shouting and outbursts of anger. Unfounded accusations would fly and ultimately the family would be drawn into the unpleasantness, most significantly my mother. She would refuse to agree with whatever had been deemed as the offense and as a result would get what she called 'the silent treatment.' These events would often occur around Christmas, Easter, mid summer and early autumn, year in and year out. My mother's way of dealing with this was to retreat to her support group of ladies at the church and her sisters-in-law who feared their brother's outbursts. She adopted the martyr roll and took on the persona of the persecuted stoic saint. I was drawn emotionally into her response on a regular basis. After about two weeks of silence dad would eventually burst into tears and be heart broken, full of remorse and make promises that this would never happen ever again, which of course it always did. I am sure his repentance was genuine but he was trapped in a cycle of behaviour that he could never break out of until the day he died. I recognised that I too had a tendency to slip into this cyclical behaviour pattern.

When I reflect on these events now from the place of being on the journey of dealing with much of my own angst and woundedness, I have a feeling of great sorrow for him and compassion and cannot begin to imagine how his life as a little boy must have been. I can only guess what sort of events he must have experienced that led him to behave in this way. I never asked him, because I never talked at heart level with him for a whole host of reasons all to do with my own brokenness and woundedness. I never knew the source of my own wounding until much later in life and I only began to get insight and healing for myself after he had died. I never had the chance to discover the reason for his pain. Sadly he took those secrets to his grave but my hope and faith leads me to believe that he is now whole and fully at peace resting in his heavenly Father's arms. However I digress.

When my mother fell pregnant with me they longed for a daughter. When I arrived I was not the girl they wanted. I was another boy and a rather naughty boy at that as it turned out.

~

CHAPTER TWO

The Naughty Boy

~

There is a school of thought that describes people's reactions to each other as 'strokes'. It is said that we all need strokes, preferably positive strokes. Positive strokes are words of affirmation, of recognition, of praise and encouragement. It is part of a basic human need. Sadly most of us don't get sufficient of these in life especially in our earlier years. The opposite is a negative stroke. These are words of discouragement, criticism, ridicule and the like. They are often cruel, hard and hurtful. Many of us recognise these and have heard them frequently in our lives and experience. Even more damaging than negative strokes, are no strokes at all. This is where a person is so ignored and devalued that nothing is said at all about them either positive or negative. It is as if they do not exist. People as a result will settle for a negative stroke because it at least acknowledges their existence rather than no strokes at all. So for me being described as a naughty boy was at least a recognition of my existence even if it was a negative label put on me by others.

It was logical that I would be dubbed a naughty boy in the

circumstance of my family life. I was not a girl and I could never be as good as my older brother. A few years ago I met someone who had known me as a child and whom I had not see for perhaps forty years. Her husband had grown up in the same church as me but was a few years older than I was. We greeted one another and her first comment was, "It's Trevor the naughty boy!" I had not heard that description for so long it quite shocked me. We laughed and I said, "I've had healing for that," but it took me back to those early days in the 1950s and my childhood home and the church culture of the Baptist Church at that time.

I can't recall when I first was given this label but stories told by my family and friends all bear witness to the fact that this is how I was perceived. Stories that were recounted were all told with good humour and fondness but nonetheless they show an underlying attitude that I lived with. One friend relates that as a toddler I reacted to the inevitable tickling under the chin by biting his mother's finger. She is supposed to have bitten me back! Stories abound of my behaviour which seem to bear out the reality of the description.

I have childhood photographs of me as a chubby, ruddy faced, ash blond, curly haired cherub. One set of pictures is a series taken, which was very common at the time, of perhaps twenty to thirty small passport sized shots. It shows the chubby little angel being held by a very tense and serious faced older brother who is clearly struggling to hold me as I wriggle and squirm on his lap. Another photo is one where I am being held by my mother and am pushing her away while my father stands beside her looking on. All this seems to confirm to me my early memories of being a difficult child.

At some point in my preschool years I was taken to see a psychiatrist for some reason. I remember being in his office and being given wooden bricks to play with. It seems that I was considered destructive. It suggests too that I was an angry child.

When I was about four years old I needed to have some sort of surgery which required being admitted to Great Ormond Street Children's Hospital in London. That was about fifty miles from where we lived. My parents took me on a Sunday afternoon and I was admitted to the children's ward. It was a typical 1950s hospital ward. There were rows of cots and beds and a central area of small tables and chairs with a number of children seated reading and playing. I joined them at one of the tables. As I settled in I glanced over my shoulder to see my parents disappearing through the double doors at the end of the ward. I immediately jumped up and ran down the ward to the double doors which were now shut in my face. A nurse intercepted me and picked me up and took me screaming and kicking back to my bed. This was a cot bed with sides that came up to stop a child from falling out. It felt like I was put in a cage. I was furious.

I know standard medical practice in that era was different and it did not encourage parents to remain in the hospital with their child. I know too that my parents believed that they were doing the right thing. I imagine they had been told that I would be fine, and they should just quietly leave and let me get on with playing. I also imagine that as the doors were closed and they walked down the corridor they would have heard me screaming and shouting. I do not believe that they were unaffected by this. They were not heartless and always did the best they could in bringing us up, caring for us and providing for us. Though at four years old I did not understand that. I felt as if they were abandoning me. I thought I was being punished for being a naughty boy. I had a very unhappy week in the hospital. I remember looking out of the windows watching people in the street, looking for my parents. The nurse that had intercepted me at the beginning of the week I called the miserable nurse. I imagine I was not an easy patient.

As I reflected many years later I began to see that this event was used by the devil to reinforce my sense of being unwanted and considering myself as a disappointment. The feeling of abandonment was very deeply embedded in my heart. I know now that probably around that time I shut down my heart to my parents. I closed off to them. It is as if I said in my heart, "If you don't want me then I don't want you either. I don't need you. I will protect myself and I will run my own life." It is as if that day I became an orphan, not physically but certainly emotionally and spiritually. I behaved like an orphan who had no parents. I do not remember ever talking at any meaningful level with them about anything. I became independent. I decided that I did not need them. Especially I closed my heart off to my father to protect myself from some aspects of his behaviour. I was afraid of him and felt continually disapproved of by him. I feared his angry outbursts and hated his silence that would sometimes go on for days into weeks. I became very anxious in these settings and at some point began to bite my nails. Little did I know what a devastating effect that this would have on my life. The devil lied to me and his lies began to be formulated into a belief system that I would live by for many years to come.

Sunday School was a major part of church life and figured highly in my experience. I had a succession of teachers over the years who were great people and did much to encourage and promote Christian teaching. On the whole these were godly, faithful people who loved God and believed their role was to serve him and particularly serve the church by teaching in the Sunday School. Sunday School was on Sunday afternoons until the 1960s when it switched to Sunday mornings. In the 1950s things were different. The mornings were reserved for the morning service which ran from 11.00am to 12.00 noon every week. At 11.30 am on the dot, all the children were marched out to Junior Church. This was because the minister was going to preach and this was for grown ups only, not children. We were shuttled off to another room for 25 minutes of terror imposed by an elderly woman full of good intentions but who presided over that short time with a rod of iron. She accepted absolutely no nonsense from any of us, especially the Naughty Boy. We sat with our backs to the chairs like ram rods and were forbidden to talk. Bible verses were drilled into us and we had to memorize them on pain of hell fire if we forgot any. She would shoot questions at us which required instant answers or else! I was not the only child to dissolve into tears at times when I was unable to give a correct response. Persistent offenders were marched back to their parents in "Big Church". This resulted in great disapproval from all as it disturbed the sermon.

This fearsome lady explained very graphically that when we died our whole life would be played back on a great big screen before all to see. Every thought, action and deed would be reviewed by God. Nothing would be hidden. We would be judged by him. I imagined that he would also test us on all those memory verses. This filled me with horror and fear. The thought of my mum seeing all this was almost more scary than God reviewing it. This teaching has been present in the Christian Church since the early third century when the first of the Western Latin Fathers of the Church, Tertullian had described God as a Judge with sinners arrayed before him in court. We were being accused before him by the devil who was the prosecution lawyer and Jesus comes as the defense lawyer who pleads on our behalf before God the Judge. Tertullian was a converted lawyer who sought to explain the Christian faith to his contemporaries using metaphors that they would understand. Whilst there are aspects of this picture that might be helpful it was taken up by Western and Roman Christianity and has become deeply imbedded in our thinking.

It was designed to give us a healthy fear of God and desire to behave and not sin. For me it did none of this. It made me think that God was one to be afraid of, who demanded absolute obedience from us with very little room for mercy or grace. God was to be obeyed. We would be judged and most of us found wanting. The naughty boy was in a crisis because God became someone on whose good side I desperately wanted to remain. All this did was reinforce my feeling of being disapproved of and not being good enough. Failure had terrible consequences. We could not wait to get out of that hall on Sunday mornings.

My family and the church were committed to the support of missionaries. Every year there was a missionary supper at church which was a great feast at which money was raised for the Baptist Missionary Society. Over the years various missionary speakers came to the church and told stories about the great Missionary pioneers of the nineteenth century, all of whose biographies were on the approved list of books that could be read on a Sunday afternoon. I devoured the stories of David Livingstone, Albert Schweitzer, Mary Slessor and Hudson Taylor and as a little boy I was captivated by the adventure and romance of these people's lives. On one occasion Gladys Aylward came to speak at our church. She was known as 'the small woman' on account of her short stature and I marveled that they put an upturned wooden orange box in the pulpit for her to stand on when she spoke. She had been a missionary in China between the wars and had finally been expelled when the Communists took over in 1950. Her story was made into the Hollywood film "The Inn of the Sixth Happiness." I was deeply impressed by her passion and desire to serve God at all costs.

In our dining room we had a missionary box in the shape of a child's cot at a missionary hospital in Congo. The box was used to collect money for this hospital run by the Baptist Missionary Society. It appeared on the table every Sunday to coincide with the weekly dole of our pocket money. The idea was that we should put some of our pocket money in it every week. It also appeared at birthdays and the expectation was that a donation of birthday money had to go in this box. This was all designed to teach us to give to God's work. Again there was always a sense of disapproval about the amount being put in the box. I always felt I never put the right amount in the box.

I deeply resented this as a child and I often looked at this box and wondered about the money in it. I would pick it up and shake it to see if the coins could be made to come back out of the slot. They did not but I found a way of opening the back surreptitiously, or so I thought. Over several weeks I was able to extract a fair amount of cash which was pocketed and converted to sweets and treacle toffee after school. What I hadn't realised was that every so often my father would empty the box and its contents were collected and given to the Missionary secretary. Inevitably it was discovered that our families' contributions had mysteriously plummeted one quarter. There was no doubt in anybody's mind who the culprit was. I was marched off to the Minister's house by my father who sat and cried as he told the Minister that I had robbed God and the poor little children in Africa. It was apparent that I now had incurred a terrible debt and I had no idea how God would view my transgression. I was the naughty boy in every way as far as the family and the church was concerned.

Our church was quite social and had a strong sense of community which was a very positive part of its expression of Christianity albeit a legalistic one. There was a rhythm to the church year that followed the Church calendar in a nonconformist sort of a way. It also followed the seasons. Christmas in both church and family life was a major event that was prepared for throughout the autumn culminating in feasting and religious festivities. My mother's preparations for Christmas began in the summer as vegetables were harvested from her extensive kitchen garden. Runner beans were salted and preserved in order to appear on the Christmas menu. In September the making of chutneys and pickles filled the house with the acrid smell of vinegar that permeated the downstairs for days. These delicacies would come out on Christmas night to accompany the cold meats which were a traditional part of the Christmas fare.

In late October Christmas puddings were prepared and steamed for hours on end. I remember that we gathered in the kitchen to stir the huge pot of Christmas pudding mixture and make a wish. It was a curious reference to ancient pagan practices but this never occurred to anyone. The puddings were all placed in basins and covered with muslin and then the steaming began. It went on for days and the end result was at least half a dozen rich dark puddings that would be preserved and used over the winter, the first making its appearance on Christmas Day. My mother's puddings were legendary.

In November it was the Christmas cake that dominated the

kitchen. It was painstakingly prepared from a recipe that my mother had inherited from her grandmother. Then into December other cakes were made. Finally in the last few days before Christmas all these preparations came to a great crescendo. Brussels sprouts always featured on the plate at Christmas dinner but these were always a source of great tension between my parents as my father hated the texture of hard Brussels. I am convinced that my mother began cooking them on Christmas Eve so that when they were served on Christmas Day they were unrecognizable and extremely mushy. It took years before I was willing to intentionally eat a Brussels sprout.

Various aged aunts, uncles and elderly friends of my parents were invited to spend Christmas. Every year there was tension in the home as at some point my father would explode with anger over someone's apparent misdemeanor. Everyone in the household was drawn into the unpleasantness and many an evening was passed in stony silence. I began to dread Christmas.

The coming of Father Christmas and his distribution of gifts for the good children was used as a major tool in ensuring that the naughty boy behaved appropriately in the run up to Christmas. The church programme was full of events from Carol services to Sunday school parties. Threats of non attendance at these events were regularly used to ensure my cooperation and good behaviour.

As the rhythm of the year continued Easter came and went amid the usual tension and upsets. The summer brought its own challenges with the annual family holiday and on a number of occasions a church holiday. These were wonderful times. I can remember at least four such events. They were held in either boarding schools or Christian Holiday homes which all had the usual collection of rules and regulations to control and manage the participants and keep everyone from having too much fun. One such regulation was the prohibition of swimming on Sundays, because this was the Lord's Day. We could swim all week but on Sundays it was prohibited because of course it became unwholesome on Sundays. It mystified me as a child why such a harmless and fun activity as swimming was banned on that day. Why did it become unwholesome at the stroke of midnight? Why did God seem to be in such a bad mood on Sundays? I never could fathom it out.

At one particular church holiday in Somerset when I was about eight years old I was pondering the unjust nature of the prohibition of swimming on a Sunday. To make matters worse it was a very hot summer and a swim would have been very pleasant. To add to the agony a number of people were sitting or lazing in the sun in the afternoon around the forbidden water. One of the Deacons of the church, the church secretary himself, was standing near the pool. I thought he was probably on "soul guard duty" rather than life guard duty. I found myself looking at him and looking at the water. As the Church naughty boy I had a reputation for all sorts of mischievous behaviour. I looked at the deacon. I looked at the water and I thought how good it would be to go swimming. The Bible talks about the pleasures of sin. I was contemplating this and decided that the temptation was just too much to bear. As Oscar Wilde once said, "What is the point of temptation if we do not fall to it occasionally?" I ran up to the Deacon and pushed him in. He hovered between the vertical and the horizontal for a moment as if in slow motion then he hit the water with a spectacular belly flop. Those few seconds were delicious and I savoured the pleasures of sin to the full. The people around the pool watched initially in horror and disbelief. Then one by one they started to giggle and laugh.

The Bible also says that the pleasures of sin are short lived and so was my pleasure in that moment. I quickly discovered something about the wages of sin which in this instance were not death but something more lingering but very close to it for an eight year old. I received a very sound spanking and was the object of my father's particular anger. I had a miserable week as a result and did some quite nasty things to people such as placing a wet face flannel in someone's bed. I think a number of the members of the church were glad when the week was over having suffered under my reign of terror.

I began to get tired of being the naughty boy. It was just too much effort. I did not like the consequences. I needed affirmation and I began to explore other possibilities.

∿

CHAPTER THREE

The Church Saint

~

At some point in my childhood I became a Christian. I remember after Sunday School one day, standing in a room with a group of two or three other children being encouraged to give our lives to Jesus whatever that meant. A key point that I do remember was having our sins forgiven which was pointed out to me were numerous in my case. This seemed very significant and I remember the teacher watching us closely to make sure we said the words. She then announced that we were now saved. I do not remember any inner conviction or experience but I can vividly remember that someone later gave me ten shillings! In those days that was about three months pocket money! Now that was significant. I also remember various people in the church coming and smiling at me and congratulating me. I liked that. It made me feel good and admired and I really liked that. Slowly a light went on in my head. Here staring me in the face was the solution to the problem of the naughty boy. I was about to become the good boy or better still the church saint or angel. I already had the physical attributes of a cherub, the ash blond curly hair which earned me the nick name Goldilocks from one rather annoying Sunday School teacher, so the spiritual and behavioral attributes were added to it to bring into life a new identity.

About six months later I became a Christian again. This time I was given a children's picture Bible, which was okay, but I would have preferred some more cash. Over the next few years I became a Christian about five times in all. Each time I felt a sense of acceptance from people which I enjoyed and hungered for. I soon became active in learning verses from the Bible by heart. One day the Sunday School Superintendent threw out the challenge that the first person to recite all sixty-six books of the Bible in correct sequence from memory would be awarded ten shillings. The following Sunday I had bagged the money. I still can rattle them off to this day. The annual Scripture exam which had not been of great interest to me now became something which I would excel at. Every year from then on I would get prizes at the Sunday School anniversary for highest marks or best attendance. These were usually Missionary biographies that were reserved for Sunday afternoon reading as of course they were considered wholesome.

Our church, like many evangelical churches had a great emphasis on prayer. My parents would regularly attend the prayer meetings. These were excruciating affairs. There were often long silences, then someone would pray. It was usually almost exactly the same prayer that they had prayed the previous week. I imagined that God needed to be reminded as if he had forgotten or had trouble with his memory. Then there were the prayers where the person praying was informing God and the rest of the church of some very interesting information that he apparently was not aware of or had forgotten. I can still remember how quiet and attentive all those listening became as some particularly gruesome aliment was described or some particularly juicy piece of news was shared with the Lord. My parents would often discuss this new information on the way home. Dad was usually quite cross that he had not been told before God had been informed. I was fascinated by various people who were apparently laid on one side in a bed of sickness. I had a rather unpleasant mental picture of this condition of people laying in a smelly vomit covered bed. One week the lady who terrorized us in Junior Church was described in this way. I hoped that this condition would last all week so we did not have to endure her regime the next Sunday. I did not say amen at the end for good measure. As it happened God must have not particularly liked her very much as she remained on one side in her bed of vomit for quite a few weeks. I began to be terribly afraid that her condition was because I had not added my amen to the usual prayers for her.

The best part was when someone nodded off to sleep. I could tell when their breathing changed and we knew they were asleep. The best bit of all was if they started to snore. It was almost impossible not to laugh, which was of course strictly forbidden in church. Usually someone would poke the offender in the ribs and give them a very disapproving look. It seemed that the Deacons, in particular, functioned well in this ministry of disapproval. I imagined that this was the main role of a deacon.

My mother was a fervent prayer warrior as she liked to be called and was active in all these meetings. The style was called extemporary prayer in that people would pray out loud without reference to a prayer book or written material. Written prayers were viewed with great suspicion by everyone in the Baptist Church. They were considered unspiritual and not genuine. At each meeting, the church attendees would bow their heads in silent prayer the moment they had taken their seats and before they even placed their Bible on the shelf in front. This was an important part of the ritual. People's spirituality was judged by the length of time and the posture adopted for this prayer. We were instructed in this behaviour at Sunday School. As Baptists we were told it was about preparing yourself before the service. I am not sure what that meant exactly but everyone seemed to do it. Great care was taken not to interrupt anyone in this ritual. Linda's Sunday School was in a Congregational Church and she was told that she should count up to ten before opening her eyes. Two family friends of my parents, who were regular visitors to our home, were of particular note because when they sat to pray they leant forward with one hand across their eyes. My father was particularly impressed with this mode. It would bring tears to his eyes whenever they came. My father would nearly always weep or at least his eyes would fill up whenever prayer featured. This could be as simple as saying grace before meals or attending a prayer meeting. He would struggle with praying out loud and really could not do it without breaking down. Very often his attempts to do so ended up in tears and this was the cause of great embarrassment. It was as if he felt completely unworthy or full of shame when it came to communicating with God. At some level I took on this attitude but it did not come out as tears for me.

In my new identity I took to the prayer meeting with enthusiasm. I was the youngest person to pray out loud at the church meeting. This happened soon after I had abandoned the naughty boy phase and had begun to refine my new persona of the Church Saint. I copied the formula of prayer my mother used. I began "Oh Lord God our loving heavenly Father, we do thank thee that thou hast......" I prayed for everything I could think of, not forgetting the poor little children in Africa whom I was particularly conscious of, having recently emptied the contents of the missionary box to fill my stomach. I also managed to think of someone laid on one side in a bed of sickness. I pictured them in their vomit filled bed. There was not a dry eye in the meeting. All the women were mopping their eyes with their handkerchiefs. My father was sniveling behind his hand. When we got home he remarked to me that next time I prayed out loud I should speak up so that everyone could hear me and that I should not mumble.

Every year the Sunday School would have a big anniversary which involved amongst other things some sort of drama or presentation. One year we reenacted the parable known as the Prodigal Son based on Luke chapter 15. I managed to land the starring role of the younger son, the Prodigal himself. This involved learning a few lines and a dramatic costume change as the son lost everything in the far country. In the rapid costume change off stage however I forgot to remove my sandals and reappeared as the returning son only to realise I had still had the shoes on. I was mortified and didn't know what to do so fled into the wings where my mother struggled to unbuckle my sandals. Finally I reappeared to great laughter and merriment. I was mortified that people were laughing at me. Matters were made so much worse when my father commented that it was typical of me to mess up the play. What a fine prodigal I was. This came back to me many years later and I felt it was, in some ways, prophetic that I had left the shoes on. The shoes were symbolic of the shoes worn by sons not servants. I look back now and see that even then God the Father was with me. The significance of the shoes became so much more important many years later.

On one occasion I was attending a C.S.S.M. summer beach mission being held in a local park. I had been invited by a young assistant Sunday school teacher who I particularly liked but I had treated somewhat badly one Sunday by my attitude and words. He asked me why I was behaving like that. He clearly was hurt by my actions. I was really shocked and sad that my behaviour had hurt someone I liked. There was a sudden realization that I had disappointed him and I felt I was a disappointment. The lies planted in my earliest days were beginning to kick in and my belief system was beginning to solidify.

I agreed to attend the Beach Mission at the park and had a really enjoyable fortnight. I can clearly remember a sense of hearing the voice of God for the first time in my heart. I felt God was talking to me. It happened one morning traveling to the Mission on the upper deck of an open-top bus that went along the seafront of the town where we lived. It seemed like God was drawing me, asking me to follow him to become one of his people. I also discovered the Bible that week in a real way. I read it for myself or rather with a group of boys who went along in the afternoons and where known as Keenites. I thought that the group was called Key Knights which sounded very dramatic and I had grand ideas about armour and swords and the like. However something was happening in my heart that I had not experienced before.

The final time I became a Christian was when I was 13 years old. It was at Boy's Brigade camp in 1966. The reality was that nearly all my life I have known about God and over the years he had been drawing me closer to him. If asked when I became a Christian I would say the first time but I know by this time (when I was 13) it was real and I not only understood what I was doing but I believed it. From

50

that day I have never looked back. Soon after that I attended classes to prepare me for baptism and in the October of that year I was baptised as a believer. I remember being deeply moved some years before when my brother was baptised and saying then to my parents that I too wanted to be baptised. They advised me to wait until I was older. As part of a typical baptismal service all the candidates were required to give a testimony which involved us explaining how and when we had become a Christian and describing our conversion experience. It was the first time I had spoken in public like this. I felt an ease doing this and I liked the feeling it engendered within me. People encouraged me afterwards and one person in particular said I should do it again some time. He was the founder of the church and was also a lay preacher. Eventually he asked me to accompany him occasionally when he went out preaching.

Along with the religious activity that accompanied my conversion I developed a strong desire to serve. If something needed to be done I would offer to help. Often I would find my way into the church kitchen and help with the drying up after some event. This always greatly impressed the people. If there was a working party planned, this was the annual tidy up of the church grounds or halls, I would be there impressing everyone with my diligence. If things like that were required at home there was another reaction. I resisted, procrastinated and would not be found when the task was needed to be done. I had learnt at home that whatever I did was not good enough or was often criticized. What I did in public at church events, others found acceptable and laudable. I was beginning to learn the art of performance and the pay off it brings in terms of acceptance. Serving began to be a default setting that was being built into my life.

My relationship with my father was never good. It deteriorated as I became a teenager.

As I reflect on this now it greatly saddens me that I did not really know him or that he did not know me. I can only begin to get a glimpse of how he must have been and what underlay why he was the man he was. I believe he loved me but he had difficulty expressing this. He struggled with many of his own issues and I felt I was an added struggle for him. People would tell me that he was very proud of me especially after I became a Baptist Minister but he was not able to tell me himself. It seemed to me that his pride was in my Christian achievements rather than in me for myself. Most of this I did not understand when I was younger and my closing off to him emotionally was as much my issue as his. It was my method of self protection that I employed as way of handling his fluctuations of mood.

My closure to him did not alter the fact that I needed to be fathered by someone. We all have need for love and affection. Recent research by a team at Oxford University which was published in July 2012 in the Journal of Child Psychology and Psychiatry found that fathers who fail to bond with their sons in the first three months could cause them lifelong behavioural problems. It studied the effect of loving contact with baby boys by their father and found that it was essential if they are to thrive. It suggested that they would be calmer and happier by the age of one. The study claims that whilst this is essential for all children it is vital for boys who seem to benefit from a strong paternal influence at a very early age. The lead researcher Dr. Paul Ramchandani suggested behavioural problems in early childhood often lead to health and psychological problems in adulthood which can become difficult to overcome.

This is fascinating research. Parents were involved in the research and did psychological tests while their child's behaviour was assessed examining whether they were fretful, disobedient, had tantrums or in the worst cases showed aggression by hitting and biting. Dr. Ramchandani reported "We found that children whose fathers were more engaged in the interactions had better outcomes with fewer subsequent behavioural problems. At the other end of the scale children tended to have greater behavioural problems when their fathers were more remote and lost in their own thoughts, or when their fathers interacted less with them. This association tended to be stronger for boys than for girls, suggesting that perhaps boys are more susceptible to the influence of their father from an early age."

Much of this struck a chord with me. This may have contributed to my life and the problems I exhibited as a child. However we are not solely products of nurture. We make our own choices and are responsible for our own lives. My hunger for the love and affection of a father was a deep issue for me. Even if I had had the best father in the world, I would still have needed something more. I did not understand that God was a Father to all of us and that he could meet all our deepest needs. That knowledge and experience would come much later in life and is the subject of the latter part of this book.

In the mean time I began to look for acceptance and affirmation from others. I was drawn to anyone who affirmed me and expressed loving affection to me. I am very grateful for many people in my early life who did this. My parents did what they could in giving loving care and provision but they struggled with a difficult child. My aunts and a number of family friends who regularly came to stay added to this. One aunt in particular unconditionally showered both my brother and me with love and affection on an ongoing basis. This continued throughout our adult lives and extended to our children. It did not stop until the day she died.

When I was about eleven years old someone who I loved and viewed as a father figure crossed a boundary. I was just entering puberty and I was subjected to an inappropriate sexual advance that left me deeply traumatized. It was inferred that I had invited this advance and that indeed I wanted it. I felt it was my fault and I was deeply disappointed in the person and myself. The lie and my belief, which had taken deep root in me, that I was a disappointment and failure and that I would be a disappointment to others was now gathering consequences that would take years to play out until finally God as a Father would arrest me and restore me.

∾

CHAPTER FOUR

African Interlude

~

Soon after going to High School a family moved to our area with a son the same age as me. They were Christians who lived and worked as teachers at a government school in Swaziland. We boys got on well and our families met and my parents, who were particularly gifted at welcoming people and offering hospitality, assisted them to find accommodation when they came back to our town two years later. On this visit back it was suggested by them to my parents that I should go to visit them in Swaziland for a holiday sometime. I was very excited by the possibilities that this would afford. This was talked about seriously and my father began investigating prices of tickets. To my amazement he found a flight that was open ended. In reality this meant that I would go for a whole year. So at the end of a rather lack lustre three years at High School I found myself flying off to South Africa and then on to spend a whole academic year at a School in Swaziland. This was an amazing privilege and a complete surprise that my parents would even contemplate such an opportunity. I was right in the middle of adolescence so if nothing else it gave them a break. My older brother went off to University that year so I imagine their life was very quiet with neither of us at home.

The whole African adventure suited me perfectly as it gave me a sense of independence and adventure. It ignited a wanderlust that was within me to travel and experience new situations and places. South Africa was in the midst of its apartheid regime and we travelled through the country on a number of occasions meeting people, missionaries and young people my own age who were growing up in that culture. Swaziland was still a colony of Great Britain ruled by a monarch and as a result was considerably more backward than South Africa. I also met District Commissioners and members of the white colonial service. The white ladies in the town were typical of the bored and pampered colonial wives of that era, living rather empty lives that revolved around playing bridge and drinking tea or gin slings in the Colonial Club of an afternoon.

I met Africans too. Boys and girls in our school, some of them sons and daughters to the multiple married, King of Swaziland. I also encountered servants for the first time. There were four attached to the household. One was a garden boy who delighted in catching and killing snakes, another was a cook who taught me how to speak some basic Ssawati and the other two house girls who washed and cleaned and got into trouble regularly with the "Missus". I loved Africa, it got under my skin and in my heart.

The academic standards and teaching style of the school were well suited to my disposition. I flourished in the rarefied atmosphere of the school. I was in Standard 8 along with about twenty others, half Swazis and the other half a mixture of races. There were only two of us in the French class and this helped me get my head around this hitherto incomprehensible language. I discovered I liked languages.

I went along to the local Anglican church on the Sunday and ended up teaching a class of children in Sunday School. I met many missionaries and was deeply affected by their lives and work. To have read about missionaries was one thing, to meet them personally and see first hand the manner of their lives, their faith and their heart for Africa, was another thing altogether. I began to think about my own life and how much I had received. How privileged I felt and how well I lived back in Britain.

Perhaps more significant than anything else I took with me was a book from the book case in the front room at home about Jim Elliott who was one of the five missionaries killed by the Auca Indians in Ecuador in the 1950s. It was called 'Shadow of the Almighty'. This book probably became one of the most important books I had ever read. I must have read it half a dozen times in my teens. The life of a young man totally sold out for God and being willing to lay down that life for him changed me. "He is no fool who gives what he cannot keep to gain what he cannot lose", wrote Jim Elliott. I copied that quote into the front of my Bible. I tried to imitate his lifestyle and began to organise myself as he did with spiritual disciplines. I started a prayer list. I would go out onto a kopie, a small hill, outside the town on a Saturday morning and pray through the list. It got longer each week and became quite a burden to work through.

Every week a letter would arrive from home. My mother wrote every Sunday afternoon sitting in her chair in the Sunday room. She never missed a week. I so looked forward to her letters. All through the year I wrote back documenting my life for her. I also kept a diary of my year in Swaziland. I planned for it to be a bit like David Livingstone and his journal, though most of my entries were far more trivial and did not involve any lions or African tribesmen armed to the teeth with spears and shields. As I look back through its pages at the spindly writing I can see a development taking place within me. I was growing up and I was beginning to focus my heart on serving God in a particular way. Without a doubt this year in Africa did me an immense amount of good. It marked a transition from being a young adolescent boy to becoming a young man.

One weekend we were in the north of Swaziland on a young people's camp. They were mostly Americans, children of missionaries, diplomats and expats. It was a very enjoyable long weekend, sleeping in tents, swimming in the river and talking late into the night around a camp fire. I do not remember the theme or content of the talks that weekend or indeed who was leading the camp, but I knew God was speaking to me. I had a growing sense that he was calling me to not only follow him but to give my life to him and serve him in whatever way he called me to serve. I began to feel that he was putting in me a desire to serve him as a missionary somewhere in the world. I did not know what that would look like or where it would be but I know it was him. I remember getting up and walking out of the tent into the night looking up at the stars in the sky, millions of them over my head. I opened my heart up to him and said I would do whatever he wanted me to do, and go wherever he wanted me to go. I felt a deep sense of him approving of me and I liked that feeling. It was different to anything else I had ever felt. I had a taste of his love and favour and grace on me and it left me feeling deeply changed. In the future I would look back to this incident as one of the moments that has changed the course of my life.

The next few years, as I sought to work out this sense of destiny and calling, would be hard as I battled with many issues and attacks that tried to divert me from this path. In reflection this may have been one of the major reasons why the following years would be so difficult. At every twist and turn of the road ahead I never lost sight of the sense of destiny that God had placed in me. In the days and months ahead I submitted my life to God for him to train me and prepare me for this destiny, this calling on my life. At the same time my life was attacked on all sides by the enemy of my soul who sought to divert me and destroy me. I recently said to a group of people most of my "stuff" happened before I was twenty and it has taken me forty years since then to sort it out and get healed. Well, I left Africa when I was fifteen. The next five years would be full of angst and teenage confusion.

~

CHAPTER FIVE

Teenage Turmoil

~

On returning from Swaziland I went back to my former High School and was moved up into a higher grade of class in recognition of the academic progress that had been made in the year away. I took up where I had left off with life in our Baptist Church. I was considered a bit of a celebrity which was interesting. People wanted me to talk about life in Swaziland. This gave me opportunity to speak in a public setting. I shared the sense of calling that was within me with the Minister of our church and particularly with one of the leaders in the church who had encouraged me before. He was a wise counsellor and from time to time asked me to accompany him when he went out to preach at local churches. He initially asked me do simple things such as a Bible reading and leading a prayer. The services were very simple in format and seldom varied. I had not "preached" but opportunity to do so in less formal settings came along.

Our church supported the Baptist Missionary Society. This organisation held annual two week long summer holidays called Summer

Schools at various venues around the country and our church youth group had regularly attended these events. Each school gathered about 100 young people from various Baptist Churches. Also two or three serving missionaries would be there and hearing their stories and catching something of the vision they carried was a major part of the Summer School experience. It was a great place to meet and get to know new friends. They were also a wonderful place to meet girls! People joked that BMS stood for Baptist Matrimonial Society. I enthusiastically attended my first BMS Summer School a few weeks after returning from Swaziland.

Church life had moved on and it was also in the middle of the swinging sixties and some of the more restrictive Christian practices of previous generations were beginning to change. Swimming was allowed on Sundays for example! We were the new hip generation who wore flares, brightly coloured shirts, mini and maxi skirts, hot pants and jeans. I acquired an ex German Luftwaffe great coat that came right to the ground of which I was particularly proud. We grew our hair long like the Beatles. Girls hair was cropped like Mary Quant or grew long like Joan Baez. We started to dance and embraced the new music. Christian songs were no longer limited to hymns and choruses. New forms of music were being explored. Guitars were the main means of creating music. We all felt very modern, very trendy, very hip.

Along with all these changes there was a subtle shift in sexual attitudes going on. The free love of the hippy movement was frowned on but not spoken against in churches. Nonetheless, changes were happening in the younger generation in churches. Relationships became more complicated as a result. Very little teaching was offered to young people to address some of these issues and in many ways churches were caught off guard by the assault that their young people were about to experience.

The following year at BMS Summer School I went as a Voluntary Helper. This worked well for me because I was there free of charge as a worker on the staff team doing all manner of serving activities. It was what I did best. All the VH's arrived a day early to help prepare the school venue. The day the school started it poured with rain and I was mopping the floor in the main entrance hall when a rather rain soaked girl came through the main doors having walked from the railway station carrying her bag in the down pour. She had a short Mary Quant crop of jet black hair, she was wearing a trendy pair of jeans and looked wonderful! What's more, I knew her. She was from my home town and was a friend of a former girl friend of mine. I had first met her the day before I went to Swaziland at a youth event put on by the local Baptist youth groups. The girl I was "dating" by letter all the time I was in Swaziland was her friend and she knew more about me than I had realised. This was Linda.

We began talking that day and it is probably true to say that we have not stopped talking since. We discovered at the BMS Summer School that we both had felt the call of God on our lives. Linda also had a strong sense of destiny and was somewhat dismissive of boys who did not share this or understand it. When we met we discovered we had a shared vocabulary and similar hopes and aspirations. By the Tuesday of the first week we were heading for more than just a walk and a talk. I remember that evening she was climbing a tree in the grounds of the school. She said later it was to get away from me. I however saw this as a perfect opportunity to help her down from the tree and as she jumped I offered my hand. She took it and I did not let go of her hand.

Those two weeks were the beginning of our life long relationship together. Within a few weeks I knew that this would be the girl that I would one day marry and share my life with. We talked about this very early on in our relationship and held on to it through the next tumultuous years of my life. We had a couple of fairly short interludes of being apart but even in those gaps we met and talked and came back together again more clear about our commitment to each other. Five years after we met we married in 1974.

One of the significant changes that occurred in our thinking was the realisation that our calling to serve God would be within a missions context. We expressed it as a missionary calling. Today the terminology we use is that of a calling to the nations. By the time I left High School that calling had been refined somewhat and my sense was that God was calling me into Christian Ministry. We were both strongly connected into a Baptist expression of church life. So it was logical that we would pursue a Baptist path which led to thinking about applying to train at Spurgeon's College in London which was the most well known and prestigious of Baptist Theological Colleges in the UK that specialised in training for the Baptist ministry. We felt that we would not be serving in Britain but overseas through the BMS and we were particularly attracted to their activity in Parana, Brazil where there were a large number of Spurgeon trained ministers working. We had met a number while at BMS Summer Schools.

In 1970 the charismatic movement began to have an impact on churches in Britain. Linda was already working and training as a nurse at St Bartholomew's Hospital in central London and was being exposed to this move of God. At home there was a similar affect going on mostly among the young people in our town. We were all beginning to hear about something called the baptism of the Holy Spirit which was very exciting. People were reportedly speaking in tongues and prophesying. All of this was very foreign and alarming to the older generation in our church who were extremely suspicious of this new teaching. Christians all over the country were discovering that the Holy Spirit was not just a name mentioned at the end of a service but was the third person of the Trinity who was as real as Jesus and who was the one who would fill us with the power of God. His powerful indwelling presence was seen as a tangible and life giving encounter which was often accompanied by great joy and manifestations of his presence such as speaking in tongues, prophecy and sometimes even physical sensations such as laughter and shaking.

Both of us were baptised in the Holy Spirit during the summer of 1971 and this set us on a different course that would only really become a major change of direction ten years later.

Linda and I were very interested by the work of Brother Andrew who wrote a book called 'God's Smuggler' and had founded Open Doors It chronicled his work into the communist world of Eastern Europe. As a result as soon as I had finished my A levels at High School, I took off with a school friend in my Morris Minor on an adventure to Eastern Europe. We were two 18 year old boys with a car full of Bibles that we were about to smuggle behind the Iron Curtain. The following year four of us went in my newly acquired VW Beetle. Linda and I and another young couple. Both these trips were full of surprises, divine appointments and a fair degree of youthful irresponsibility. We learnt to trust God and step out in faith in many ways. We encountered a Christian Ministry in Austria that was working in Eastern Europe who took us seriously, gave us some common sense training and prayed us off as we headed east. We met Christians in Romania, Bulgaria and Yugoslavia whose life and testimony challenged us. For Linda and me this was our first major foray into the world of Christian missions. Linda's gift of languages served us well as she had studied French, German and Italian at school. She could also helpfully say, "The cup is under the table" in Serbo Croat, particularly useful when asking for directions in Belgrade.

To train for the ministry I was encouraged to start preaching and again the local church assisted in this by encouraging and testing my calling. I left school and went to work for a year at a Rehabilitation Centre run by a Baptist social mission that owned a large country house. This centre known as Greenwoods, was called a therapeutic community where people with all sorts of problems and disorders lived together and were encouraged to explore and overcome their individual issues. This was mostly done through non directive counseling and group therapy where people expressed themselves if they wished. It was all rather vague and waffly and I am not really convinced it achieved very much long term change. However at the time it was popular. It exposed me to all manner of people whose lives were very different from mine and took me out of the protective bubble that I had been in. It also exposed me to unhelpful influences that hooked those needy and unhealed parts in my own life. This was not something I was aware of at the time.

The community was divided into two groups, guests and staff. I was staff along with about a dozen or so others. There were about thirty guests.

Towards the end of my year there I was approached by one of the guests. He looked me in the eyes and said, "You are not as innocent as you look either!" This comment hooked a deep insecurity in me and I wanted to know what he had seen in me. We talked late into the night with devastating consequences. I was deeply shocked at this encounter and the next day I talked to Linda about what had happened. We began to recognise there was a vulnerability in my life that needed addressing but we had no idea how to deal with it or where to go to for help. We had no meaningful language to describe my inner turmoil that was triggered by this incident.

I developed a coping mechanism for my angst and any unresolved issues. Where sin occurred I did what the Bible required. I repented, confessed it to God, asked for forgiveness. I was always particularly drawn to the story of the prodigal son in Luke chapter 15 and identified strongly with the younger son. I would, like the boy in the story, come to my senses and return home with the speech carefully prepared.

> *"Father I have sinned against heaven and against you. I am no longer worthy to be called your son, make me as one of your hired servants."*

Except of course I misquoted it, and did not address my statement to the Father but to God. I missed the point completely about relationship with the Father. I also did not really consider myself a son. What I really said was, "God I've sinned again, I'm so sorry, please forgive me. I feel so unworthy. I will try harder not to do this again and I will work so much harder for you if only you will forgive me." All of which of course is not what the Bible teaches but what many of us have believed for so much of our Christian lives.

Once this mantra had been established I added a load of self condemnation and shame and the lies of earlier years and the resulting beliefs deepened. The lies were deeply hidden roots that I was not conscious of. The beliefs that drew their energy from those lies were like a tree trunk that was growing up and becoming part of who I was and how I thought. Events and circumstances such as the one at Greenwoods became like branches of the tree that grew off the trunk. These branches produced fruit which were the sinful actions, thoughts and emotional responses. I would sink into despair and shame feeling a failure and a disappointment. Sometimes these reactions gave way to periods of depression and deep sadness. I had no idea how to deal with these emotions and responses. So the solution I came to was to bury them. It was as if I dug a pit or constructed a cellar in my life where I deposited these things. I securely closed the cellar door and made sure everything stayed locked away and out of sight. This was particularly important because I was about to embark on four years of study and training to be a Baptist Minister at Spurgeon's College in London.

~

CHAPTER SIX

Training and Texas

~

Spurgeon's College was the most prestigious and evangelical of the Baptist Churches' training institutions in Britain in the 1970s. It was a great achievement to be accepted at Spurgeon's. Only those with a clear and tested call to ministry were accepted and I had applied as a missionary candidate which meant my intention was to serve with the BMS in Brazil. On that basis I was accepted. I was 20 years old.

Linda and I had become engaged in February of that year on her twentieth birthday. This was a particularly special day as she is a leap year baby and it was a leap year. I entered college however as a single man. Girl friends and fiancées were considered an entanglement by the Principal. It was a very male dominated institution. Our year group of twenty students included the first two women in the College's history. It had the feel of a men's boarding school and theological students had a reputation for much silliness and childish behaviour. Linda at the time was working on the cardiac ward at Barts dealing with real life and death situations on a daily basis and found my schoolboy like behaviour more than a little irritating at times.

Within weeks of starting at the College tensions began to grow between us. Not only my juvenile student behaviour but also the inner tension that had accompanied me when I went to College contributed to this. The prodigal-like cycle of behaviour continued and I sank into a deep pit within the first month of starting. On one level I was an enthusiastic new student enjoying much of the study and life of the college. On another my inner life was in continual upheaval lurching from one crisis to another. The result of this led to me breaking off our engagement. This hurt Linda deeply and we both withdrew from contact with each other for several months.

During the months that we were apart I was a total mess. I formed an unhealthy emotional attachment to another student that was causing me great anxiety and pain. It played to all my insecurities and unmet needs and left me more wounded and with more stuff to cram into my already over crowded cellar. The College did not have a pastoral structure for students so there was no one I could turn to for help. In reality, it was probably the last place I would have gone to for help as it would have meant I would have felt exposed and I greatly feared that happening. I remembered how I felt as a child when I was publicly humiliated for my mistakes and failures.

After several months of struggling I finally went to see my local GP and he referred me for counseling to a psychiatrist at a large London hospital. To my great relief after a few sessions of talking the psychiatrist confirmed to me that he was a Christian. However, that was after a series of sessions involving some form of aversion therapy which included the administration of electric shocks all designed to recondition and set up new responses in the neural paths of the brain.

It was totally ineffective and quite embarrassing and unpleasant. He felt my issues were spiritual rather than psychological and that the best help would come from the Lord. At this point I was discharged and left to get on with it. The visits themselves and the opportunity to talk had done much to lift the depression and gave me the resolve to work through some of the immediate consequences. It did not begin to get to the root issues. It would take many more years for these to be dealt with.

I contacted Linda by sending her a huge bunch of flowers on her twenty-first birthday. A few weeks later we met again and picked up talking where we had left off. She told me that she and her closest friend and flat mate had been praying for me throughout the previous months with quite remarkable insights. Her feminine intuitive gifts had discerned with startling accuracy much of what had been happening to me. Within a very short time our love for each other was rekindled and we renewed our commitment to be married. I had completely turned away from my previous destructive behaviour pattern and had been through a major prodigal experience and homecoming with an even greater desire to work harder and be a servant of God. We both had however a new and better understanding of what that commitment would involve. There was a new openness between us that was a great relief. We were married the following year in 1974 in our home town by the minister of Linda's church and Bryan Gilbert her former pastor came and sang at our wedding. He had led us both to faith in Christ and had baptised Linda and her family.

During the early part of my time at Spurgeon's many of the students were secret Charismatics. Officially the College did not countenance such views but a number of us would regularly attend meetings in London that featured such speakers as Bob Mumford, Charles Simpson, Derek Prince, Ern Baxter and Arthur Wallace. This was at the beginning of what began to be called the house church movement which evolved in time into Apostolic teams lead by Bryn and Keri Jones, Terry Virgo, Gerald Coates and others. There was something very clandestine about going to these meetings at the Bonnington Hotel in Central London which, as young students, greatly appealed to us. It sowed seeds into us that would eventually grow and take root and would transform our theology and practice of church life. We were introduced to prophetic teaching and ministry and we heard some of the men whose teaching would impact not just church life in the UK but the shape of late twentieth century Christianity all over the world.

During the third year at Spurgeon's I became the Missionary Secretary. As I was a missionary candidate I was automatically given the role. The task involved inviting a missionary speaker every Friday morning to come and address the student body. I invited a wide range of people from all types of missions to come. One of them was a middle aged woman whose father had founded the European Christian Mission. Her address to the students gripped my attention as she talked about the immense challenges of the continent of Europe. It became apparent to me that there was a huge mission situation much closer to home than Brazil. This was the start of a growing interest in the need for mission activity in mainland Europe. Our visits to Eastern Europe had introduced us to some of this need and now in the remaining years at College I began to shift my attention more to Europe. By the time I reached my final year, Brazil had lost its appeal and Europe was beckoning us. We neither felt ready or able to go straight into a mission situation there. We were sensing the need to gain experience in a church somewhere closer to home first.

As it happened a situation did open up but it was far from home. Spurgeon's had an arrangement with First Baptist Church in Dallas Texas whereby every year one of the graduate students would go to be an intern at the church. The intern concept was unknown in the UK. In my final year the Principal asked me if I would consider going to Dallas. I hardly had to think about it. The only problem I saw at the time was our son had been born during that last year and it would mean taking a nine month old baby. Enquires were made and enthusiastic replies were received from Dallas. So we began to prepare for a year in the USA.

Just before leaving for the US we had the graduation ceremony from Spurgeon's and then my ordination as a Baptist Minister. This was held at my home church. Many of the key figures who had helped us to arrive at this moment took part in the ordination. This included Bryan Gilbert who had shared in our marriage. As I knelt and had hands laid on me setting me apart for the ministry to which God had called me I felt very inadequate for the task given my age and experience. However I was excited and full of anticipation for what the future would hold. My life had settled down as marriage and parenthood had given me responsibility and great joy. The prodigal cycle had receded into the background and I did not think very much about what was buried in the cellar. I began to feel that time was a great healer. However the roots were still in place. That did not occur to me on my day of ordination. I looked across the crowded church at faces that I had known all my life. Finally my eyes rested on my parents. My mother's face glowed with pride. She now had a son who was a Minister. My father's face however was hidden by his handkerchief but I could see his blood red eyes full of tears. He never said anything to me that day. Somebody told me that he was so proud of me. I imagine that may have been the case but he could not express it in his own words to me. There again that was nothing new.

The year in Dallas was wonderful. We loved First Baptist Dallas, we loved Texans, we loved the USA. We felt like celebrities especially as we had an absolutely adorable little boy, our son Nick, with us who was the star of every show. The Texan ladies queued up to get a peek of the little Britisher as they called him in the nursery on Sundays. There were over four hundred under threes in the nursery so he was a bit of a novelty.

The Church functioned on a typically Texan grand scale. It was huge in every way. It's membership was over 18,000 of whom more than10,000 were regularly involved. The sheer number of buildings in the heart of downtown Dallas that it owned was amazing, spread over eight city blocks. They said that if they were all put on top of each other it would make a sixty-eight story sky scraper. I had hardly come across a church with a car park let alone a six story parking garage, a roller skating rink, a gymnasium, a basket ball court and a six lane bowling alley. Being part of such a great church was very exciting. President Ford visited one Sunday. Billy Graham was on the membership, several of the Dallas Cowboys Football team were members. Each service was like a professional concert with a seventy piece orchestra and a three hundred voice robed choir that entered the sanctuary every Sunday singing a stirring version of 'On Jordan's stormy banks I stand." It was pure theatrical drama that thrilled and overwhelmed and wowed the crowds.

There was also a depth to the people in their love for God and in their larger than life attitude to everything. They had an understanding of God that involved a great love for Jesus, a passion for the church, a longing for revival, a desire to serve, a generosity of heart, wonderful southern hospitality and incredible optimism. This was totally different to our experience of Church life back in Britain. However they were scared stiff of the Holy Spirit and all things charismatic. They were extremely parochial and had little understanding of life outside of Texas let alone life in the rest of the world.

My main responsibility was to speak, in as fluent a British accent as possible, at every possible opportunity. The most public opportunity was exhibited every Sunday morning at both services where I had to deliver the offertory prayer. This was to last no more than one minute and was to include at least one intercession and mention the words tithes and offerings. Furthermore the posture for prayer was a kneeling pose of one knee on the ground the other for supporting a sincere hand gesture and was to be spoken into a bowl of flowers beside the lectern. The flower bowl concealed a microphone so that all four thousand worshippers present and those watching on live TV could catch every carefully intoned and crafted syllable. I drew deeply on my childhood memories of prayer meetings and I had an extensive repertoire of the "prayers to make 'em weep' variety. So I was a roaring success. They even recorded a tape of my prayers that was sent to one of the old people's homes!

The pastor of the church was Dr. W.A. Criswell who had been pastor since 1948. His predecessor was Dr. George W. Truett who had been pastor since 1898. Dr. Criswell was an old school pastor the like of which is rarely found now. In his youth he had been a fire and brimstone preacher and he had retained much of that passion and fire in his preaching style. He was a very interesting character who managed a large staff of over one hundred and twenty people very effectively. One of my tasks was to do hospital visitation and my allotted day was Wednesday. On any given day there would be perhaps forty people in various hospitals scattered across the city of Dallas. The biggest concentration was at the Baylor Baptist Hospital. On a Wednesday afternoon I would make my visits. The idea was that everyone in hospital got a visit each day from one of the pastoral staff. Not a long visit but a short one which had to include a brief prayer. My prayers were in particularly high demand because of the accent. So usually I had to make at least twenty prayer stops each Wednesday afternoon. Generally patients were in single rooms which meant for privacy. One afternoon on entering a room there were two patients in the room and the one on my list from First Baptist was asleep. The other who I spoke to was from First Methodist. We chatted briefly, I prayed and left first checking that my lady from First Baptist was still asleep.

On returning to my office I found a note on my desk from the Pastor's secretary. Dr. Criswell wanted to see me the minute I returned from Baylor. I went straight to his office wondering what this was about. His secretary greeted me and whispered "You are for the high jump my lad. Sister Harrison was not asleep!"

Dr. Criswell's office was a cross between an antique emporium and a room from Buckingham Palace. He invited me to pull up a chair beside his ornate mock Louis XV desk. We sat next to each other and then he pulled open his desk draw. To my amazement it was full of unshelled peanuts.

"Help y'self son" was all he said.

We shelled peanuts for a couple of minutes in silence throwing the empty husks into his gilded antique waste paper bin. Then he paused as he picked out another and the conversation went something like this.

"Have you been to Baylor today, son?" he asked in his deep gravelly Texan drawl.

"Yes Sir," I replied in my carefully enunciated Queen's English.

"Did you pray for them all?"

"Yes Sir, with exception of Sister Harrison who was asleep."

"Well, son, she wasn't asleep, just restin' her eye lids." There was another long pause. "Have another peanut , son. She was on the phone before you got to the elevator. She was sharing a room with a woman from First Methodist and you prayed with her, I understand?"

"Yes sir."

"Good to pray for them Methodists, surely Lord knows they need it, but you should have prayed for Sister Harrison. So, listen son, the last sense that goes before they die is hearing. So always pray for them, even if they are in a coma or if they are fakin' it like this gal was."

"Yes sir."

There was a long gap as he looked at me with a twinkle in his eye.

"Have another peanut son? You are doin' a good job. Now get on home to your sweet wife and that cute little bugger of yours."

I should explain that 'little bugger' is a term of affection in Texas with nothing derogatory about it at all. What amazed me about Dr. Criswell was he always called me son. I never felt patronised by this. No one had ever called me 'son' before and I found it initially slightly odd but quickly grew to like it. However I had no idea how to be a son to anyone because I had the lost the heart of a son many years before when I closed my heart to my Dad. He never called me son. His term of endearment all his life was to call me 'boy'. I disliked being called that intensely.

One person who also had a significant impact on us was a lovely Texan woman in the church called Mary Crowley. She was a kind and generous woman. She was a multimillionaire having established a huge business empire in the USA based around selling items to decorate and beautify the home. She used the system of getting home based young mothers to hold demonstration parties to sell her products. Mary was not only a highly successful business woman but she was also a generous hearted woman with the spiritual gift of giving. She gave away millions of dollars over the course of her life. She gave so much that at one time she was investigated by the American Tax authorities who did not believe the amount she claimed to have given away. She was thoroughly investigated and totally exonerated. Mary would not throw money around but she would listen to the prompting of the Holy Spirit as to how, when and to whom she should give. Some years after we left Dallas she would hear from God and give to us at a moment when we needed money.

Towards the end of the year in First Baptist I had the opportunity of preaching at both Sunday morning services. This was also broadcast live on the local TV station. The main point about this was that I chose to preach on the Great Commission based on Matt 28:18 - 20. This sense of calling to the nations was growing deeper in us as the years went by.

We left Dallas at the end of our year having had an amazing experience that changed the way we thought about church and how I would act as a pastor. We had been such a success that Dr. Criswell offered me a job to stay on to join the staff of the church. I was very tempted as we both really loved Texas. Linda was pregnant with our second child and we felt that we should return to the UK to seek a church position there. We do wonder how our life might have been very different if we had stayed in the US. However we both agreed that we needed to go back to Britain.

~

CHAPTER SEVEN

The Italian Job

~

On returning to the UK in 1977 we began the process of finding a church which would like us enough to invite me to be its pastor. The Baptist system was very straight forward. It all boiled down to whether people liked the way you preached and if they liked you. After a couple of weekend visits and if you had preached a good sermon they would all have a meeting when the members would say what they thought. Then it was down to a vote at the Church meeting. A majority vote and you are in. Anyway we received a unanimous call from a church in Hertfordshire on the day our first daughter, Susannah, was born. We moved to Berkhamsted a couple of months later and at age 24 I was responsible for the pastoral care and spiritual leadership of a group of 60 or so people. I look back on that now and am amazed at their courage at taking me on especially as I sported a very unusual wardrobe of very Texan suits!

We had nearly five very happy years at this church and after two years our second daughter, Christina, was born completing our little family. The church grew throughout that period to over two hundred and fifty members. Much of the growth were converts and new people moving into the town. The links with First Baptist Dallas continued and we had a couple of evangelism teams come from Texas which created a strong bond for a few years between the two churches. Mary Crowley came on one of the teams and her visit to the church had a significant affect on a number of business people in the community. Our personal link with her also deepened.

The church was committed to supporting overseas missions which we encouraged. They prayed regularly that God would raise up missionaries from within the church family that would be sent out to the mission field. During our time there we continued to think about our own interest in overseas missions. We had a growing sense that our own future involved some sort of work abroad. We started to develop an interest in Italy. In reality our connections with Europe and particularly Italy had grown through a friendship with a leader of a new Charismatic church in our home town. We had known Chris since we were young Christians and we had watched as he had moved from a gathering of friends into what was known as a house church. We continued to be attracted to this expression of church life though we had no personal experience of how to lead a church like that. We were firmly in the Baptist mould but were beginning to feel somewhat restricted by the democratic system of church government that characterized the Baptist church. There were great people in our church but our desire to flow more in tune with the Holy Spirit was becoming an issue for some of them, particularly those of the older generation.

As Italy began to figure more on our spiritual radar so too did the desire to be open to the work and ministry of the Holy Spirit in our lives personally and in the church. Eventually we talked with the leadership of the church about our growing interest and conviction that we were considering joining a Missionary Society that worked specifically in Italy. This was not a denominational society but a faith mission which meant we would need to raise our own financial support rather than be centrally supported by a denominational society such as the BMS. We did not know it at the time but this was part of the plan that God had for us that would lead us out of the Baptist Church into a different expression of church life. That journey has not ended yet and continues to this day.

The church and members that we were leading in Berkhamsted were very supportive of us if a little surprised at the choice of Italy as a missionary situation. The mission we were drawn to was non denominational and in the UK was open to charismatic influences, at least in theory. We made formal application and were accepted as missionaries for Italy. They were impressed by our somewhat limited pastoral experience and felt that we would be ideal to lead a small team to regenerate a tiny group in Trento in northern Italy and replant the group as a church. I had absolutely no idea how to do that but was excited nonetheless.

As part of the testing of the call to Italy I contacted our friends Chris and Margaret who had links there and they suggested I attend a conference in Italy organised by an emerging group of Italian charismatics. The theme of the conference was about the restoration of New Testament values and teaching to the church. I travelled to Rome and then by train to somewhere near Firenze for a three day conference. The speakers were Keri Jones and David Mansell who were key leaders in the emerging house church group that became known as Covenant Ministries led by Bryn Jones.

The teaching on the conference was unlike anything I had come across or heard before. The meetings were accompanied by Spirit led worship and prophetic ministry that I had not experienced since the days when we sneaked out of Spurgeon's to attend meetings in London. I felt in many ways that I was coming home to something familiar and which I deeply wantedto be part of. Most importantly I made connections with Italian Christians who were radical in their expression of life and church. It sealed the deal as far as Italy was concerned. This was where we believed God was leading us to next.

We left the UK in the summer of 1981 bound for Perugia, Umbria, in central Italy to begin a year of language study at the ancient University for Foreigners. We packed up our home and set off in our VW Camper van with our little family as missionaries to Italy. The last thing we did before we left was to visit our friends, Chris and Margaret, who were part of the house church movement and who had strong links in Italy. I remember saying, "I don't know quite what I mean by it but we feel we want to ask you to cover us when we are in Italy." Chris said he would think about that and come and visit us soon after we had set up home in Perugia to talk further about covering us.

The Mission had given us a contact in Perugia but apart from that we were on our own. We had visited a few months before and had stayed in Trento with a couple from the Mission who had been on their own there for three years. Leaving our wives and children for a few days this guy and I went down to Perugia where we would be based for the first year to look at possible places to rent. We got on well together superficially but I discovered that he was a Calvinist who believed that all that was required of him was to preach the gospel and the Lord would bring in those who were predestined for salvation. This was going to create a few challenges because I had a very different approach to evangelism. It also explained why there was just him and his family in the church in Trento.

We arrived in Perugia and thanks to the great help of the couple who ran the CLC book shop in the city we secured a flat to rent in a village just outside thecity. Our landlord and his wife were people I could write a book about and were Italian versions of Dickens characters. Signor Stoppini could not pronounce my name so I told him my middle name was Paul, from then on I was Signor Paulo! His wife Maria Pia, which literally means Pius Mary, taught us a very colourful collection of Italian vocabulary that I could never use in church.

We enrolled our children in the local village school. They spoke no Italian but within one month Nick was speaking well and by Christmas was fluent which is more than can be said for his parents. We started to navigate our way into Italian life and culture and turned up at the church recommended by the Mission on the first Sunday morning. We discovered this to be a Brethren Assembly which, of course, was not open to anything to do with the Holy Spirit as we understood it. We also discovered to our alarm that the Mission had neglected to tell us that they worked closely with this branch of the church in Italy. In our introduction over the coming months to Italian Protestant church life we also discovered that there was very little contact or relationship between the few denominations that existed in Italy. If anything there was hostility and suspicion. We found this out later but only after we had met and become friends with the Dutch leaders of the local Assembly of God Church in Perugia. For the whole year while we were in the University we attended this church and had a very happy time. Each week was a nail in our coffin as far as one couple in the Mission were concerned. At the end of the year unbeknown to us they circulated a letter to all the Brethren Assemblies in Italy warning them about this new English couple and our serious Pentecostal affiliations. This was our first encounter with the seamier side of Christian attitudes; sadly, it would not be our last.

After two months in Italy we received our first official contact from the Mission in the arrival of a post card hoping that we were settling in well. A month before, our friend Chris from the UK had made a personal visit to encourage us, see our new flat and spend time exploring what "covering" might mean. I think we were beginning to experience it a little as it included relationship and care. We so appreciated his several visits over the next year as he always included us on his itinerary when he came to Italy. Every visit enabled us to talk and gain a greater understanding into the way God was restoring lost truth to the church. This truth that had been known in the beginning but had been forgotten over the centuries and which was now being given back to the church. The charismatic renewal that was still growing around the world was beginning to be more grounded in biblical truth. There was a growing and developing understanding of the place and purpose of the fivefold ministry gifts of the Holy Spirit, apostles, prophets, evangelists, pastors and teachers that are mentioned in Ephesians 4.

A number of men within the emerging house church or new church movement were being described as apostles. Perhaps a better description would have been that they had an apostolic ministry because the word or title apostle was causing great concern in traditional parts of the church not least within the Mission of which we were part. Instances were being reported of individuals wielding great influence in these new churches and that many personal decisions had to be submitted to the local eldership for approval. This was, somewhat inaccurately, called heavy shepherding. Certainly in some cases this may have been true but it quickly became a useful catchall to label anyone who spoke strongly into a person's life especially if it was not welcomed by the recipient. The term preferred by them was 'to speak into a person's life.' This described the process and the openness of heart to one another that was so different and attractive in these newly emerging churches. There was a reality and honesty that was both refreshing and disarming at the same time. This became problematic when individual responsibility was taken away and where there was no freedom to discuss options and come to a different conclusion than the one the local eldership or apostle were proposing. We had yet to experience any such negative aspects of this from within the house church movement. We were increasingly being drawn into this stream during our time in Italy.

The year of language study passed quickly and towards the end we met with the Mission leadership who came down from Kandern in Germany to discuss our move to Trento where the church was to be replanted. I was asked to lead the team which included the couple who had been living in the city for three years and an Italian who had lived in the UK and was returning to Italy as a missionary. We were scheduled to move to Trento in August. We found an apartment to rent and moved north with great expectations.

In an attempt to engender a sense of team and relationship between us I encouraged the two team men to accompany me to a conference being held by the Italian 'restoration' or house church group. My friend Chris would be there and importantly, Keri Jones one of the so called apostles of the new movement. In hindsight my naivety at thinking this would unite us as a team was extraordinary.

It was a wonderful conference in my opinion but by the end was viewed with great suspicion by the other two. On returning to Trento we began to make plans for relaunching the little church. There were supposedly a group of people who had been part of the group there over the previous few years. It soon turned out that they had dispersed for a number of reasons. We also started to talk together about the values that we would teach in the new church. The Mission's official policy was that those who gathered would determine the nature and style of the church. My view was that people would become what we had taught them. So it seemed important to agree as a team what we would be teaching them. We agreed on the need for salvation but we avoided the methodology because our Calvinist team member had a very different view to the rest of us. We agreed on believer's baptism in water by immersion as we were all from a Baptist background. Then I raised the issue of the place and role of the Holy Spirit and in particular the baptism in the Holy Spirit as a separate experience from conversion. Throughout this time I was not clear in my own mind and was leaning towards a second experience theology rather than an initial identifiable and distinct experience as part of the becoming born again process that is more biblical. There was a need to clarify my thinking at some point but events overtook us and that had to wait.

Our beliefs about the Holy Spirit were quite contrary to the others on the team and this very quickly degenerated into the forming of two camps. Within a month it became apparent that we would not be able to agree over this issue and that we needed to inform the Mission leadership of developments or rather the absence of developments in Trento.

The ensuing months were painful and disappointing. We were

told we were unwelcome in the other team members homes. The letter sent by other missionaries earlier in the year warning people of our heretic views surfaced and soon we found ourselves very much on our own. I used these months to write a paper on the Baptism of the Holy Spirit. This was not for any other purpose than to ground what I was thinking in a more biblical foundation.

Eventually I was summonsed to Kandern in Germany to meet with the Mission board and explain my position. Ever with a sense of drama I felt like Martin Luther going to the Diet of Worms!

I met with the board which was made up of about ten men from across the Mission leadership. It was clear that I would be questioned about my views on all matters relating to the Holy Spirit, charismatic teaching and practice, our vision for the church in Trento, the place of Apostles and so on. They sat in a semi circle and I was placed in a chair facing them. It was a very hard experience. I was grilled, roasted, and turned on the spit! The bottom line which was presented to me was to turn or to burn. I had never experienced anything like this before. I was unprepared for the intensity of the questioning and the coldness of the atmosphere. The proposal being put to us was that we should keep our charismatic views to ourselves. If we felt the need to speak in tongues we should do so in private. We should not promote or encourage any of the controversial gifts of the Spirit and that in all our public communications we should not make any reference whatsoever to any of these issues nor teach them in the church. I had discovered in the previous weeks that the US branch of the Mission was strongly supported by dispensationalists who did not believe that the gifts of the Holy Spirit were for today and that they had effectively ceased when the New Testament was written. The strong support from the USA was financial in nature so our stance was considered a great threat to this.

The alternative for us was that we should resign from the Mission if we felt that we could not abide by their conditions. Confronted by this august body and the emotional pressure that was being put on me was too much. Linda was not with me to talk to, she was back in Trento with the children. I needed space and time to consider. So unlike Martin Luther I did not have my "Here I stand, I can do no other" moment. I had a "I can't handle this!" moment. I took the train back to Trento through the Alpine tunnels and felt I was descending into a very long one. I had found myself having to explain and defend a view of church of which I had no first hand experience. My answers were all theoretical and lacking in conviction not born out of first hand knowledge. Yet we had tasted something in our spirit that we longed for and we were facing a significant life changing moment of decision.

When I got home Linda and I talked long into the night. After two days we contacted the Mission and informed them of our decision to resign. We also contact our home church in Berkhamsted and our friend Chris. Within two days friends from the church were with us to support and encourage us, bringing not only comfort and contact but Marmite which really impressed the children. A week later Chris was with us and we were exploring what we believed the Spirit was saying to us about our future.

We agreed together that we would not leave Italy or Trento but rather we would stay and connect on a regular basis with a new church that was part of the Restoration movement as it was now called in Italy. This church was just outside Venice about two hours away from Trento. We agreed that we would explore together what God was saying about our future but we believed it was to stay in Italy for the time being as independent missionaries. We also had to address the issue of our financial support so it was decided that we would return to the UK over the Christmas to talk to supporters and friends.

The visit was not the easiest as there was considerable disquiet among those who had offered us support because of our connection with the Mission. Most of these understandably cut their financial support for us. Others, however, increased their support. We returned to Italy after four weeks in England feeling that God had been doing a more significant work than we had realised. He had taken us out of our comfortable Baptist world and launched us on a journey that we are still on today. We resolved that we would follow him whatever the cost and our desire was to not settle but to move on whenever he moved and to whereever he would take us. This was and remains our hearts desire and very much set the course for our future and ministry ever since. I did not realise that at some point it would involve opening the cellar and dealing with the stuff deposited there. That would happen quite some time in the future but was an essential part of the refining process that he had begun in me.

On returning to Trento, I got a job teaching English at a language institute. Linda began working as a volunteer in the hospital in the city. We also travelled every other week to Mestre, Venezia to be part of the church there. The next six months were hard. At times we felt very lonely and disconnected. Our Italian wasn't brilliant and we did not always understand the subtleties of what was being talked about especially in the church context. We loved the people but I clearly did not know how to express what was happening to us and was not in a place to offer any form of leadership. Old insecurities resurfaced and I felt a failure and that I had disappointed so many. Eventually we decided after discussion with Chris that we would return to the UK and become part of his new church which was part of Covenant Ministries. We felt we needed to belong to a group who believed and behaved in the same way as we were wanting to do. We wanted to experience this and learn from this in a context where it was functioning. So we returned to the UK to our home town.

The last thing we did in Trento was not really connected with us personally but was part of something else entirely. There was no functioning Protestant church in the city. The one we had hoped to be part of did not materialize either. From my studies of Church History I knew that the Council of Trento, which had been a major part of the Catholic Counter Reformation in the sixteenth Century, had met over a number of years in the Cathedral in Trento. At the end of the Council the Catholic Church had listed a number of Anathemas or effectively curses on many of the basic teachings of the Protestant reforms. A classic example of these Anathemas is the curse on anyone who reads the Bible in any version other than the Catholic Latin Vulgate version. Some of these have since been changed by subsequent Catholic Councils. However, I had been unable to find any specific references to a lifting of these curses. So Linda and I went to the Cathedral on the day we finally left the city and prayed that the power of these curses be broken. Especially, if in anyway, they had prevented the establishment of a Bible believing community of Christians in the city that this power be broken. We prayed for a sense of Christian unity to come to the city. Many years later we were encouraged to hear that there were several churches along with the Roman Catholic church in the city.

～

CHAPTER EIGHT

Covenants and Tea Cosies

~

So we returned to the UK. We had tried hard to hang on in Italy. However in many ways we were broken by the experience. Particularly because this was our first experience with such major differences of practice and attitude among Christians. It was the challenge of doctrinal belief and the intransigence that shocked me most. The inability to find a way of accommodating differing views and at the same time maintaining some level of relationship was very difficult to accept. The reality of the power that money had was also deeply disappointing. Soon after we returned we read an article in the Mission magazine which reported our departure from Italy as being because we no longer had Italy on our hearts. This was particularly hurtful because it was blatantly not true and was a convenient cover up of the real issues. A number of years later when looking at the Missions website and reading an article there about the beginnings of the church in Trento I found another reference to our departure and this time it was put down to theological differences. This was much closer to the truth.

There were theological issues at the root of it but they were not just cold doctrinal issues, they were heart issues that we were beginning to believe passionately. We believed that we were at the forefront of a new move of God in our generation and like many in the past there had to be a choice and a willingness to lay things down that we had once held dear in order to take up the new and move on with God. We felt we were like the early American pioneers who had crossed the Appalachian Mountains and were heading down the Ohio Valley in search of a new land and a broader horizon. My study of church history if nothing else, had taught me that each new move of God was very often opposed by the last. I have seen that the worst persecution came from the last persecuted group rather like the Swiss reformer Zwingli persecuting the newly emerging Anabaptists in Zurich in the Sixteenth Century. He had them drowned because they wanted to espouse adult baptism by emersion. In a small way we felt a little persecuted especially by colleagues in the Mission but also misunderstood by friends and family who were solidly rooted in the Baptist tradition. One of the deacons at our former Baptist Church commented that we had simply got our guidance wrong and we needed to get over it and get another church.

We did not feel like that at all and we decided that we would not return to the Baptist Church but we began to attend the Covenant Ministries church in our home town. They welcomed us with open arms, prayed and prophesied over us and did all they could to encourage us and help us settle back into our old town which we had not lived in for ten years. My parents were particularly unhappy and disappointed because in a few short months I had gone from being a Baptist Minister and Missionary, albeit not with the BMS, to a disgraced and theologically confused former minister and missionary in their eyes. They had no paradigm in which to place this change. To be fair to them I did not discuss any of this with them because I did not discuss anything of any consequence with them. They just got the headlines reported to them. I felt their disapproval and disappointment.

Interestingly, my brother who did not move in any Christian circles made an astute observation one day. He thought it would probably have been easier for them if I had become a Jehovah's Witness! At least that way they would have known what they were dealing with. Whereas they just did not get this charismatic thing. For the rest of our church life my mother could never bring herself to call the churches we were part of a church. They did not qualify in her mind. She referred to them with a hesitation in the middle, "Your, err, fellowship." That was the best she could come up with. I think she tried to understand but she was very much held back.

We so much wanted to experience the freshness of the revelation that we had begun to discover in Italy. We started to look for somewhere to live in the area of the town where most of those associated with the Covenant Ministries church was based. We had no money and no job. Linda's family helped in trying to create a job for me within the family business but I was definitely not a precision engineer.

We felt however we should try to buy a house. We had no deposit and no means of obtaining a mortgage. I saw an advertisement for a sales position with a company selling insurance. This was in the days before financial regulations had been imposed on the industry and just about anyone was taken on. It was commission only and they offered basic training. More to the point they offered a mortgage scheme based on projected income. I was offered a job and off I went for two weeks induction and training in the company portfolio of Insurance products and financial packages. Suddenly I was a financial consultant! This was very scary and I am embarrassed now when I think back on all those friends who bought insurance from me. I guess they mostly did it out of sympathy for us. It's the classic approach for all commission only jobs, hit your friends first and you are bound to get some sympathy sales. Then when you struggle and leave the experienced sales people pick up all your friends as clients.

We took up the offer of a mortgage and I sold the appropriate life cover to myself! All that was needed was a house and a 10% deposit. We found a house in the area where most people from the church lived for £30,000, a mid terrace in a reasonable part of town with a good primary school up the road. This was going to be important as the children had just had two years in Italian only schools and their playground English wasn't up to much. The girls from time to time would converse with each other in the dialect of their nursery school in Trento which none of us could understand.

We began to pray for the 10% deposit that we needed. We had no idea how we would ever raise £3,000 in time. We were about to withdraw our offer when we had a letter from our former church in Berkhamsted. They told us that Mary Crowley, from Dallas had sent a cheque for us about two months before by sea mail because she had heard from God that she should send us some money. God told her to send $5,000. However her gift had strings attached. She specified that it was for our accommodation needs. Two months before when she sent it we were packing up in Italy with no idea of buying a house. When it was cleared through the bank and through the church account it came to £3,300. We received it with open mouthed astonishment and joy. We were even able to tithe it and gave our friends Chris and his wife £300. We did not know that they had asked the Father for a new bed and had found one that cost £300 and they like us had no surplus. We were learning about God's provision for us when we step out in faith on the journey with him.

We moved into our new home with a sense of great anticipation for what was to unfold in the days and years ahead. We discovered there were a few others in the church who had come on a similar journey out of traditional church situations. This was encouraging to us and we became firm friends with them. We all joined what was referred to as 'The Commitment Course.' It was a weekly gathering of people like us who had joined the church. It was designed to help grasp the teaching and values of the church. This was a good system and throughout the process we were partnered with another couple in the church who helped us process the material and helped us as we integrated into the church. This was essentially a very good idea. After a while one or two things were said that I found a little concerning. It became apparent that everything in our former Christian lives was considered as dead works. This was particularly true if, like us and another couple on the course, we were formally full time Christian workers or pastors. I can understand where they were coming from but I was not convinced that all of my Christian life and experience before this time was of no value and should be regarded as dross. I still believe that Father has us on a journey and we live in the grace and light of each day but we do not camp there. We grow and move on but we are the sum of our life and our past.

We carry it all with us, good and bad, positive and negative. God uses all of our experiences to mould us into the people he wants us to be. Certainly there are things that are not biblical and ungodly in our lives and our pasts which it is good to leave behind and press on into the new. This is where we found ourselves and these were things which we were now embracing.

The church which we became part of was a rapidly growing community and eventually divided into two halves at either end of the town. This meant that more opportunities to serve opened up. Before long we were home group leaders and occasionally I preached at a meeting. We had regular visits from the leaders of Covenant Ministries who were described as apostles, the brothers Bryn and Keri Jones. They were on the look out for potential leaders as their group of churches were multiplying rapidly across the UK. As a result we were invited to various prophetic weekend events for all these potentials. They were curious gatherings. Perhaps 150 to 200 people gathered at each event. There was teaching and ministry but the main part was to wait to be prophesied over by one the movement's leaders who were deemed to be prophets. These men, and they were all men, prowled around the room during sessions looking intently at people during worship and teaching times. Then at the end of the session certain individuals were called forward for a prophetic download. It all became very intense. Soon it engendered a competitive attitude among people because the ones prophesied over were deemed to be specially selected or anointed. It was bizarre. Some of those people were then taken off and within a short time news circulated that they had been asked to move to a new church setting. After some time we also heard that those who had not felt personally called to move in agreement with the apostolic and prophetic directive were marginalised and were described as having an "unteachable spirit". Some as a result were put out of fellowship, which meant that they were now persona non grata as far as Covenant Ministries was concerned. It was things like this that were happening which began to ring a few warning bells to us and some others in our church.

Our church had one such prophetic visitation and the leader, our friend Chris, was asked to move to another part of the country to lead a church. We all supported him in this move and wished him well. He was replaced by a team of emerging leaders from within the church. This worked well for a while. Then there was a large event planned in a local concert hall which was to be addressed by one of the apostles of the movement. It was designed to be a dramatic demonstration of God's Power as people were healed, delivered and saved. This would be seen as a demonstration of the anointing on this particular apostle and a validation of his apostolic credentials. We all planned and prepared and packed the venue with people. There was a great amount of hype and excitement but at the end of the evening there was no evidence of anyone being healed, delivered or indeed even saved. Nothing was publicly said about this it was just acclaimed as a jolly good time by the local leadership.

That was not the feeling among many in the church. People started to question the lack of manifest power displayed and asked questions of the leadership. This was not the required response and very quickly the church was informed that to question like this was unacceptable and a sign of rebelliousness. This created more reaction among people. At the same time as this was happening a directive had come from the Apostolic team that all women would be required to wear 'head coverings' in all meetings of the church. Whilst some had done this as a result of their own personal convictions, for others this requirement was considered an imposition of a non essential practice. Non compliance was considered symptomatic of a rebellious spirit. Husbands whose wives did not comply were deemed to be failing in bringing godly leadership in their families and were, as a result, not fit for leadership and in themselves were failing as men. Consequently the women of the church began to comply and wore a variety of creations. None wore old fashioned hats, mostly it was head scarfs or berets. Occasionally something which resembled a knitted tea cosy appeared much to most people's amusement. These were soon censured when it was realised that the bizarre nature of the head gear was itself a challenge to the whole ridiculous idea. Eventually this silly practice was abandoned, thank goodness but it came at a time when questions were being raised.

These various issues eventually came to a head one weekend when the embattled leadership instructed all the lower levels of leadership of the church to present themselves and their wives on a Monday evening at the church office to personally swear their loyalty and reaffirm their commitment to the leaders of the church. This was very sad as it had been such a good church in so many ways. The overwhelming feeling among people was that church was not meant to be like this. The behaviour being exhibited and demanded was coming from a place of insecurity. Much later we would describe this sort of thing as orphan like behaviour. This evening began to be referred to as Black Monday. It was the beginning of the end for the life of the church.

Soon after these events yet another prophetic visitation occurred and the leaders were replaced and the ring leaders of the dissension dealt with. Some left the church. Others were encouraged to move on to other churches in the network. We came into the latter category.

I had left the Insurance company after about ten months as I had run out of friends willing to buy products from me. However I had discovered that I liked selling. I looked around for other openings and a job came up working for Avis Rent a Car, a major international company. I became a Sales Executive with a company car. My territory was the West End of London around Mayfair which was very up market. Over the next three years, I was promoted to Sales Trainer, then Sales Project Manager. The motto of Avis is 'We try harder' which was perfect for a performance driven, orphan hearted servant like me! I excelled at this. Meanwhile, we were encouraged to move to the Midlands by Covenant Ministries to be part of a large church in Leicester. I told my boss at Avis that I was leaving the company in order to move to Leicester because of our involvement with church. He was initially incredulous! Then a few weeks later he offered me a position in the company as Sales Development Manager, a role he created in order to keep me in the company but which would allow me to live in the Midlands. A few months after moving my boss was made Sales Director and he in turn promoted me to Southern Sales Manager based at Heathrow. This involved a daily commute down the M1 or a flight from East Midlands airport. This was complementary as part of a deal Avis had with British Midland. It worked very well for me and reduced my travel time to a little over an hour. I was quite the jet setting young executive and rising star!

The sense of favour I felt while I was working for Avis Rent A Car was extraordinary. After a year as Sales Manager I was promoted again to National Accounts Manager responsible for the ten top UK accounts which included IBM, British Aerospace and Marconi. I was rapidly going up the corporate ladder. It was also beginning to take up increasingly more of my life. Corporate entertaining was great fun in the boom years of the 1980s. Visits with clients to Wimbledon, tickets to the Centre Court, away days to the races and even a weekend which Linda was able to join at Scotland's top luxury Hotel at Gleneagles were all part of the activity. However Avis wanted me body and soul and that is not what I wanted.

Ever since leaving Italy we had wondered what God wanted from us in ministry. The few years in the Covenant Ministries church had taught us so much and we were very appreciative of this. It had changed our approach to so much of church life. Moving to Leicester broadened this understanding but it became apparent that we were not on their radar as far as any form of ministry was concerned. I don't think it was ministry for ministry's sake that was behind this. We both felt we had a destiny and we also never lost sight of the call to the go to the nations, but we had no idea how that would happen. I remember sitting in my expensive company car outside an IBM office in Portsmouth on my thirty-fifth birthday wondering and asking God if this was what the future was. Did he want me to be a Christian in the corporate world or was there still a call on my life for some sort of full time Christian ministry? I was open to either, but in my heart there was a desire to serve God and particularly to be able to work out in a church context what we had been learning in Italy and subsequently within Covenant Ministries.

I don't remember how it happened but I had contact from a friend one day who asked me about these things. He was in a national Christian leadership position and was aware of a number of churches that were looking for some sort of trained full time leadership. I told him I was more than open for this. In the end two situations presented themselves and we began to consider them seriously. The first factor that hit us was the income issue. I had a very good remuneration package with all sorts of perks from Avis and could afford all manner of holidays and luxuries. We had two good incomes between us as Linda was working as a School Nurse and earning good money too. The prospect to returning to a fairly basic income at a time when the children were about to become teenagers was a challenge. We went away for a very wet week in West Wales to talk and think things through before we agreed to seriously consider either option.

Two weekends later we were in Norfolk for a long weekend visiting one of these churches. Three weeks later we were back in Norfolk and at the end of the week we had received an unanimous call to be the Pastor of the church. It was not a denominational church as such as it had recently experienced a move of the Holy Spirit which had led them to become independent. It was however small and enthusiastically open to the Holy Spirit and to whatever God want them to do.

I went back to work the next day and my boss asked me to come to his office. I had done nothing wrong, instead he was burbling on about all sorts of new opportunities he wanted me to take on and dangled a big carrot of a huge pay rise before me. I stopped him and said there was something I needed to tell him.

He said, "I know you are leaving aren't you?" I was surprised.

"You are going back to the Church aren't you?" Now I was stunned.

"How did you know?" I asked him.

"I couldn't think of any reason why you would go to Norfolk for two weekends like you have unless you had something like that on the cards. All this stuff about pay rises etc, I knew you wouldn't be interested. I know this is not what you really should be." I was really stunned!

He was not a Christian but he could read people and he could read me.

A month later we moved to Norfolk. The leadership of the Covenant Ministries church we were attending said we were stepping out of the will of God, being rebellious and that God would not bless us, nor would they bless us if we left. We were breaking covenant and we would be under the judgement of God as a result. Again we were on the receiving end of heavy shepherding.

We understood why this group were so often accused of this. Many had left this movement as a result. It was a great shame as there was so much promise and so much that was good, radical and biblical about it. I have never given up the sense that God is restoring lost or forgotten truth to his church but I know it is not to make a new denomination out of the new or recovered revelation. I know that not everyone will see the new thing or be willing to move into the new but many will. In moving to Norfolk we did wonder though whether we were taking a step backwards because the church we were going to was still very denominational and religious in its ways. At the same time we had a strong sense that this was a door that God had opened up to us.

~

CHAPTER NINE

New Horizons

~

We so enjoyed moving to Norfolk. The seven years we served at this church in Norfolk would be some of the best and most satisfying years of our lives. They were very successful years but partly in this were the seeds of my subsequent crash. Success carries a price and has many pitfalls attached as I would discover especially when so much of my identity was locked into being successful.

Over the years we slowly built a foundation into the church that reflected where we had come from and where we felt God was moving. We had a strong and clear group of leaders and people who passionately wanted to go wherever God would take us. We could not have achieved all that was accomplished without this dedicated and godly group of people. The Church had grown out of one of the splinter groups that emerged in the Nineteenth Century from the fragmenting Methodist church. It was essentially a very rural church in a small county town where nothing much went unnoticed. For its size it made a much greater impact on its community than a similar sized church in a big town would have done. This is good and bad. Good news and bad news travelled equally as fast. When they severed their Methodist link this caused more than a few waves in the religious community. Pews had been removed along with the old wooden pulpit from the chapel building that they owned. I enquired of one of the elders what had happened to the old pulpit and he told me he had taken it to his farm. There was a look in his eye that told me there was more to this than he was letting on. Next time I was at his farm visiting him and his wife I asked if I could see the old pulpit. His wife giggled and he looked very sheepish and replied in a wonderful broad Norfolk accent that I could not see it because he had burnt it. I was in the presence of a true twentieth century iconoclast! This man was a pillar of the church. When he prayed in a service the whole spiritual level of the meeting was raised considerably. He had the gift of faith which took the church forward into new realms of life and progress on more than one occasion. Without people like this dear man and his wife the church would not have been the church it was.

One of the early needs that the church identified was to belong to a wider body of Christians. The Church was part of the Evangelical Alliance but that was not a strongly relational grouping. It had its place in the nation but was of little consequence locally. Soon after moving to Norfolk I heard that a much older man than I, who had also trained at Spurgeon's, had moved to the county and had started leading a church in Norwich about the same time as we had. He was a part of another of the apostolic groups that were growing across the country. This group was also committed to the restoration of New Testament values and truth to the church. They saw the church as the primary agency that God was using to bring salvation to the world. They shared many of the values that we had been growing in. It was a fairly easy step to start meeting together regularly, with one or two other pastors and leaders from across the county who shared similar values and hearts.

Slowly and steadily we began to connect with this network of churches. One of the features that so impressed me was the sense of relationship that existed between the leadership. This group said they were friends and they acted like friends. There was not the same intensity of control that we had experienced before. Their emphasis arose very much out of the background of its leaders in a more reformed evangelical tradition as well as one that is very open to the Holy Spirit, the prophetic and apostolic. A number of them had been there at the Bonnington Hotel meetings back in the early '70s and had continued to grow in influence over the ensuing years. As a church we agreed together that we would join this network and this greatly added to the vibrancy of the life of the church and its place in the wider body of Christ.

The church grew over the years in every way, numerically and spiritually. In one year there were fifty two conversions of unchurch people which felt like revival! Our children grew into teenagers in the church. We loved the fact that we were in rural Norfolk. Norwich was far enough away not to be a big pull when they were in their early teens. The church had an active youth group which, over the years, was a very important part of the life of the church and was excellent for our teenage children. They all benefitted greatly by being part of the church. One of the first additional staff members that joined the church was a Youth worker. We rented the local high school and community halls after we had outgrown the old chapel. We were all feeling that it would be good to have a building suited to the needs of the growing church family. Some weeks later a semi derelict building in the town came up for sale. I remember walking around it one day and looking at it. Was this destined for greater things? It was possible.

We talked and prayed and shared the vision with the church. We commissioned a local architect to draw up some sketches about what could be possible. Then we presented them to the church. Together we realised that God was opening up another door of opportunity and we agreed together to make an offer on the property. Within a few weeks the deal was done and then the real work began of renovating and adding to the structure to create a centre and that would house a variety of activities that were in the hearts of the people. Eventually it was officially opened and we were delighted to announce to the assembled hall (which was full with nearly five hundred people) that we were debt free. Every penny had been raised by the people of the church themselves.

Staff were added and soon we were seeing over 300 people gathering every week to worship. We planted a church in another town. We had students based with us and were sought out by other churches. I was gathering other pastors and we were being looked to for advice and support. Some were even saying that I was functioning apostolically. On one occasion we hosted ITV's weekly Songs of Praise act of worship which went out live one Sunday morning on national TV. We were making waves, we were becoming known across the county and in the wider Christian world. We were becoming known in the network of churches of which we were part.

In the midst of all this success I was feeling old issues beginning to resurface. I did not realise the extent of these damaging thought processes. With all the acclaim I nonetheless felt lonely. I desperately needed the recognition. It made me feel validated and affirmed. In my heart I was insecure and struggling. My parents showed little interest and occasionally asked how things were going at 'your, err, fellowship.' I wanted to be on the inner wheel of the network of churches. To be recognised by the leadership. I remember coming back from a couple of days away when we had gathered with other leaders to pray, driving though the dark country lanes planning a Reggie Perrin like disappearance in which I just went missing and where everyone would think I had died. I wondered if anyone would care. I was very self absorbed and I imagined Linda getting over it quickly and finding someone much more suitable as a husband than I felt I was. As a husband, I did not feel a success. All manner of irrational thoughts were swirling through my mind. I was on a spiral that was nose diving out of control.

I covered all this up and put it in the cellar. The very fact I was thinking like this, together with all the stuff from my early years made me think more about all these issues. I had bitten my nails for years and in my morbid introspection I was trying to work out why. John Wimber came over from the USA and led a conference in Brighton. His influence was very significant in the UK at that time. At the conference I had found myself falling to the floor weeping and weeping with no understanding why and for what. Someone who was praying over me said it was unblocked grief that was coming out. Grief over what? I had no idea. I kept all this inner turmoil to myself. I did not share it with Linda or anyone else. I did not know who to share it with and I was afraid of opening up. I was afraid of exposure and public humiliation so I decided to do nothing. On the surface I was a successful leader, inside I felt a fake.

Sometime later, soon after my fortieth birthday, I was in London for a meeting and stayed at an older friend's house overnight. I had known him for years and I decided to share my inner struggles. I thought he would have insight into these things. We spent an evening talking and chatted late into the night. Then the unthinkable happened again and we crossed a line that I deeply regretted. I sinned morally. In hindsight I think I knew at some level that this might happen. I knew I was walking on thin ice and that there was the potential for disaster. I was looking for affection and affirmation from an older father figure all over again. It was history repeating itself.

When I went to my room in the early hours of the morning I cried for many hours. I was in deep shock and full of self loathing and shame. All the demons of my youth came rushing back to assail me. I had opened a door again that I thought was shut long ago and I was in deep despair. I felt a complete failure and was desperate. I cried out to God that night and poured out all my fears, my pain and my sadness and sin to him. By morning I left after expressing deep and heartfelt regret for what had happened. I accepted my own culpability and responsibility for the events of the evening before.

I went home and I told no one. I went though the prodigal cycle and vowed that I would try harder and I was extremely hard on myself. I felt forgiven on one level but I did not know God as a loving Father. I only knew him as a God who I was afraid of and in whose presence I felt great shame. I had covered myself with the fig leaves of being a successful and well-liked pastor who was creating a reputation for himself. I served God partly out of fear and with a desire to be acceptable to him but also because I genuinely wanted to serve him with my whole heart.

So I told no one and I opened the cellar door and dropped in more of my stuff. I closed it as tightly as I could and got on with what I knew how to do best. I served God. I hoped that if I died I would hear him say, *"Well done good and faithful servant, enter into the joy of your Lord.*" If I died in a bad week it was anyone's guess what I would hear.

The bizarre thing about all of this was that I taught and believed in forgiveness, mercy and grace, in confession of sin and repentance. I would regularly quote 1 John 1 verse 9

> *"If we confess our sins he is faithful and just*
> *to forgive our sins and cleans us from all*
> *unrighteousness."*

We all believed this in our group of churches. It was one of the things we valued and encouraged. I now recognise that much of this was a theology, a teaching that is thoroughly biblical and applies to us when we are saved, which we believed at a head level as conceptual truth. I am not sure if we really believed it at heart level, however I did not make that a distinction then. As the saying goes, 'You don't know what you don't know!' Whilst we had great compassion and mercy for sinners needing forgiveness and grace it was not clear, because it was not talked about, whether this same degree of grace would be extended to Christians who fall into serious sin after their conversion. What about those who supposedly should know better such as church leaders? Was there grace for them? Would there be grace for me?

After a few weeks went by I did not notice any less blessing on the work we were doing. I certainly felt contrite and was probably more humbled. I interpreted the blessing in my life as an indication of forgiveness and acceptance by God. Slowly I began to breathe again. The weeks turned into months then years and the cellar door stayed firmly shut.

CHAPTER TEN

The Toronto Experience

~

Early in 1994 a rumour began to circulate that there was some sort of revival going on in Toronto, Canada. I mentioned this one Sunday morning in a message I was preaching. Suddenly I found myself weeping as I spoke. I was expressing a deep longing that many of us felt in Britain that the church would be revived and that this would lead to a change in the Nation and a turning back to God on a major scale.

A few weeks passed and more reports were circulating that what was happening in Toronto was an outpouring of the Holy Spirit in an unprecedented way. People started to go to Canada from the UK to find out what was happening and to assess whether this was a genuine move of God. Nearly all the reports coming back were positive. What was also surprising and interesting was that people returning from Toronto appeared to bring the influence and the affect of this outpouring back with them and it was beginning to impact their own churches in similar ways.

What was happening in a small Vineyard church in Toronto was about to change the course of many thousands of people's lives for ever and ultimately the shape of church all over the Christian world.

The beginnings of this move of God go back to the 1970s. An American itinerant preacher called Jack Winter had been preaching and teaching a message about God as a Father. This was nothing new doctrinally but what was distinct about his teaching was that he believed that the love of God as a Father was not just a theological statement believed by all Christians but a tangible expression that could be experienced at heart level. He taught that knowing God as a Father was not just an intellectual concept but was an essential experience for all Christians. Knowing him in this way was the key to living the Christian life because we would know we were accepted and loved at the very deepest level of our beings. This experience would bring healing to our broken and wounded hearts. He taught this for a number of years. Jack would hold people in his arms representing the Father to them and praying a simple prayer,

> *"Father let my arms be your arms and,*
> *Father, come and pour your love into*
> *this person's heart."*

Many thousands of people were touched by this ministry.

Jack Winter was made particularly welcome within Youth With A Mission (YWAM) who opened a door to his ministry. He was joined for a few years by a young couple from New Zealand, James and

Denise Jordan, who travelled with him and ministered this teaching across the USA and other nations. They eventually returned to New Zealand and took this revelation of the Father's love with them.

In the course of his travelling ministry Jack went to Ontario, Canada and was welcomed into a church led by a couple who had experienced a move of God in their church. As Pastors, they were not sure about some aspects of this outpouring and had as a result shut it down. They subsequently felt that they had quenched the Spirit. When Jack Winter visited them he shared with them the revelation of the love of the Father and they began to see that when the Holy Spirit was poured out it was a gift of the Father's love and an expression of God loving his people. They promised the Lord that if ever he graciously did this again through their ministry and church they would not quench it but would welcome all that Father wanted to do. This couple were John and Carol Arnott who, in 1994 were pastoring Toronto Airport Vineyard.

When this new visitation from the Father began in Toronto, Jack Winter was one of the first to visit and became convinced this was a genuine outpouring of God. The Toronto church very quickly called this outpouring the Father's Blessing. As news of this spread in the UK a number of prominent and influential churches such as Holy Trinity Brompton began to experience similar manifestations amid the outpouring. The British tabloid press began to write reports and dubbed it the 'Toronto Blessing'. Jack Winter contacted James Jordan in New Zealand and urged him to go to Toronto and see what the Father was doing. James flew to Toronto and had an incredible encounter with God. On the plane home to New Zealand he reports that he shook as wave after wave of the Holy Spirit swept over him. On returning to his church in Auckland, as he stood to share about the week in Toronto, the power of God fell on the church and the Father's love began to be poured out.

In the UK we heard about the revival and the move of God. Some of the leaders of our network came back from a visit and gathered as many of the leaders as they could for two days to share what was happening. As they explained what had happened to them and what God was doing wave after wave of the Holy Spirit's presence was unleashed across the room. For the next two days over five hundred leaders and elders were overwhelmed by the power of God. I was there with a group from our church in Norfolk. We like everyone else were deeply and powerfully touched. I do not recall any mention of this being the Father's blessing. It was described as an outpouring of the Holy Spirit. There were unusual expressions or touches on people. The most common was laughter. It seemed to be the most natural thing to do as an expression of joy came up from deep within. There were tears and groaning and "sighs too deep for words." There was a weight that overwhelmed people and they fell to the floor under the power of the Spirit and remained like that for many hours as God's Spirit seemed to be doing some deep work within them. In some cases there were bizarre manifestations that were inexplicable. Many, after several hours of this, were like drunk men and there were reminders of the description of the disciples on the day of Pentecost in Acts 2. The whole event was similar to descriptions I had read of revivals and outpourings in the past such as the Cane Ridge Revival in the USA in 1802, and the previous moves of God associated with Jonathan Edwards and the Wesleys in the eighteenth century. To be alive and experiencing this in my life was amazing. I knew that we were experiencing a moment of church history in the making.

After two days of this we went back to our churches across the country and like wildfire these outpourings continued. The next morning we gathered our staff team to tell them what had happened and we sent messages to the teams at the church plants to come to the meeting. As soon as we started to share the Spirit began to move among us and for the rest of the day we were all overwhelmed in this incredible presence of God. Word spread and soon church members were coming to the church to see what was going on and by the evening large numbers had gathered and were encountering God. This was right across the age range of the church and the usual activity of the church was suspended as God was doing his work.

The next Sunday was to have been the first of a series of six seeker friendly services. We had been looking at the approach that was attracting many people in the US particularly at a place called Willow Creek. This involved removing from the services anything that un-churched people would find embarrassing and culturally unusual and to communicate the gospel in a seeker friendly way. We had been planning for these six meetings for weeks and had a very good team of gifted people who planned drama, interviews, special musical items and songs. We had donuts and coffee as people arrived and the presenters sat on trendy bar stools and held hand microphones. It was brilliantly done. Many people arrived including a large number of seekers and the un-churched. The problem was that in the prayer meeting before the service most of the church were on the floor or rolling around laughing in a very non seeker friendly way. How we got through these mornings without embarrassing anyone I have no idea. We were remarkably controlled. After six weeks we had received a great deal of positive feedback but no one got saved or started attending the church on a regular basis.

During the evenings on those Sundays what was usually a smaller gathering turned out to be huge. Everyone came hungry for God and desiring to worship and enjoy his presence. We had two worship teams planned for the evenings because usually the first team didn't manage to get through the first song or two before they were a heap on the floor or laughing uncontrollably. We seldom managed to preach but many people were being transformed. People who had drifted away from church life were touched and found their faith renewed. People brought friends and some were so overwhelmed by the power of God that they got saved. They were extraordinary days. People started coming from all over the county and from other churches to meet with God.

In November 1994 a group of us went to a major prophetic conference held by Toronto Vineyard. It was rather like a school boys outing but we had a very enjoyable time. It was particularly good to see and hear first hand what was happening there. Also it was particularly good to listen to John and Carol Arnott as they sought to explain and come to terms with the extraordinary events that had overwhelmed them. One of their team was a church historian who skillfully put this move of God in a very clear historical context. The church in Toronto were struggling to manage thousands of people coming to receive and experience the Father's blessing. Plane loads of Koreans came for the conference. There were perhaps four to five thousand in attendance. There were things that were strange and there were people who were enjoying the ride. The accusations that it was all 'in the flesh' were not without some foundation as there was clearly some of that going on at one level. That is true in almost every church situation. However, undeniably there was a definite dynamic that cannot be explained in any other way than this was a sovereign move of God.

Back in our church in Norfolk this went on for the best part of two years with varying degrees of intensity. Throughout this whole time, I laughed. This was significant to me since I seldom laughed especially when touched by the Spirit. I usually cried when the Spirit touched me. But this was a season of laughing for me. On one occasion as I rolled on the floor laughing I found myself at Linda's feet. There were another pair of feet next to her and I looked up and recognised the feet of a local Anglican vicar. She said to him that this had to be God because I was not one to laugh like this.

One weekend in the middle of all this fun and games we had a phone call from my parents. They had seen a deal in their newspaper offering very cheap bus tickets for the coming weekend to anywhere in the country. They announced that they would like to come to us for the weekend. This was truly remarkable as they usually avoided coming to us for a Sunday because it would mean coming to our 'err fellowship'. They had only done this once or twice in the past before things had become really crazy. They had found it so culturally different from the safe Baptist Church in their sleepy retirement town on the South Coast. I tried to warn them that things were fairly unusual at the time and maybe they would prefer coming during the week. The special ticket specified that it could only be used over a weekend so it was set they would come for the weekend. As a parting question my mother asked, "Will you be preaching dear?" How could I begin to explain! I said, "Maybe". This confused her somewhat so I just said we would explain it all when they arrived.

They took the bus as planned and we began to try to explain what had been happening over the last few months. They seemed incredulous and had really no understanding of what we were talking about. Sunday morning came. Each week we had a pre-service prayer meeting which served to set the tone for the main meeting. There were so many crammed into the side hall for this meeting that hardly anyone was in the main meeting hall. My parents were sitting in there with a few others stoically awaiting the meeting to begin. There were some people in our church who took perverse delight in praying for such an anointing on the speaker or leaders that it was virtually impossible to get out of the room and into the main meeting hall. This was one of those days and I was meant to be speaking. I was plastered!

Eventually I made my way into the hall for the start of the main morning meeting. I was very wobbly but at least I was on my feet and not crawling on my hands and knees. The worship began and we didn't get through the first line of the first song before the keyboard player was so drunk in the Spirit that his finger got stuck on one note. He was gently removed and the second team took over. It was total Holy Spirit mayhem. After about twenty minutes I climbed back on my chair and looked across the church. There was a group of elderly ladies slumped together laughing with tears pouring down their faces. I saw a pair of legs waving in the air between the rows. There were bodies all over the floor and in the aisles. A couple of younger people seemed to be pogo sticking in the corner. I spotted my parents sitting in the middle. My mother had her handbag clutched on her lap held by white knuckled fingers and was staring at a spot on the wall in front of her. My father was flicking through his Bible. I guess he was looking for the verse about doing everything decently and in order. I can't remember if I preached that day.

Over lunch we discussed the price of potatoes, the weather, the latest news of the aged aunts but absolutely nothing about the service.

To my amazement they wanted to come back in the evening even though I said I probably wasn't preaching. The evening made the morning seem quite tame. At around 9.00pm I suggested to Sanna that she might like to give her grandparents a ride home in the car. She told me later that they had asked her if our church was usually like this. She apparently replied "Oh no Grandma, it's usually a lot more wild than that!"

Early in 1996 I was reflecting on the previous eighteen months in the life of the church. I think I was sitting on the floor at the back one Sunday evening surveying the lines of the bodies of people receiving and doing business with God. I was enjoying this move of God immensely. It was particularly remarkable that the intensity was not diminishing and people were not tiring of it. The joy and lightness that was a feature was still wonderfully refreshing. I had been reflecting on this for some weeks, but inside I had a deep pain that was always there. I struggled with a foreboding that I could not define or put words to. I felt the Lord speak to me. Surprisingly what caught my attention was that he used my name.

He said, "Trevor are you enjoying this?" I laughed again and said, "Of course I am enjoying this. It is the most amazing time".

I particularly felt that I must be really forgiven if God was blessing us and visiting us like this. I answered him and then I heard him say,

"Good. I am so glad, now are you ready to let me deal with your stuff?"

My first thought was, "What stuff?"

However I knew exactly what he meant. My cellar was stuffed full of my stuff. I had been cramming stuff into my cellar for years. I pondered for a while, not laughing now, then the tears began to flow.

"Yes, Lord. Whatever it takes."

I wondered what it would look like or feel like to let God deal with my stuff.

What did he mean by my stuff? I thought about the things I had put in my cellar. I could draw up an extensive list. All these things on my list I felt ashamed of, I felt disappointed about. I did not recognise it very clearly then but I felt I was a disappointment and I felt shame in myself not just about things I had done. These were two of the things on God's list that I was not aware of. It would take time for these to work their way to the surface.

Fundamentally I did not know who I really was. When you don't know what you don't know life is far less complicated. In many ways that describes where I was at. I did not really have any idea what was on God's list. I was focusing on my list. It would gradually dawn on me over the coming months and I realised that I didn't know who I was or indeed who God was. I was looking at him through Adam's fallen eyes. It was as if what he was saying to me was, "Trevor, where are you?" My reply was just like Adam's reply, "I was afraid, because I was naked, so I hid." I was at the start of a new phase on my journey in which I would come out of hiding, tear off the fig leaves that had covered me, all my false identities that I had hidden behind and would begin to look into the face of God, no longer afraid but looking into his loving eyes and seeing him as a Father who really loves me.

To get to that place involved an incredible amount of pain and that was just around the corner.

~

CHAPTER ELEVEN

Disclosure

~

What was I to do about this invitation from God? I thought about this for a couple of weeks and became progressively more unhappy. It was as if the longer I left it the more uncomfortable I felt. It was as if the cellar door was open and I could smell the stench of years of unresolved and unhealed rubbish. Finally I decided that perhaps I should talk to someone and ask them to pray for me. Above all I wanted this to be a private and confidential time that would satisfy the criteria of "dealing with my stuff."

I made a tentative enquiry of a fellow leader in another church in our network as to whether he was willing to have a serious chat with me about some issues. He agreed to meet me and I drove over to the town he lived in. I knew the guy quite well and we had shared a number of ministry situations together over the previous few years. What's more we had spent many a happy hour laughing on the floor together under the influence of the Spirit.

We met and I began to open up a little. He shared some of his issues which reassured me to be more open and more explicit about

FALLING FROM GRACE INTO GRACE

the nature of my problems particularly in my childhood and teenage years. We prayed and he agreed that we should talk again. This time he came to my house one morning. We sat across the room from each other and I told him about what had happened about four years ago. I noticed a change in his voice and face as I shared. He asked if he could pray for me. I agreed. He crossed the room and came and sat beside me and put his hand on my shoulder to pray. Suddenly I was filled with panic and fear. I had been in a situation like this before and was desperately afraid. I jumped up and stood by the fire place. I asked him to not touch me. I did not accuse him of anything inappropriate because I am sure his intentions were godly but both he and I were very shocked by my reaction. After a while he rose to leave and said that my situation was far more serious than he had first realised and that he would need to ask for advice from the wider leadership team to whom we were accountable. He did not ask for my permission, he just announced that is what he would do and said he would get back to me.

Incredible fear gripped my stomach from that day. It churned inside and left me feeling exhausted and upset. My fear was exposure and I was about to be exposed. I had just told someone about the most shameful thing in my life and he was now going to tell someone else.

Within days things began to happen and I discovered I was unable to do anything about it. I felt I was hurtling towards an oncoming train. Shortly after this a close friend who I had known since the days in Covenant Ministries, and who was now leading a church in a nearby town, came to see me. He had been briefed by the other leader. So we went for a walk to discuss what was likely to happen. It turned out that the senior leadership of the network had already been briefed also and it was decided that the elders of our church needed to be informed and that some sort of disciplinary action should be taken. It became apparent that I would have to tell Linda. My emotions were in utter turmoil as my greatest fear was becoming a reality.

I so wished I had not agreed to deal with my stuff. This was too much. We talked about the possibility of a sabbatical. This is often used to cover up some sort of difficulty. I thought maybe a six month leave of absence would be a possible solution so I could get some professional help.

A few days later I broke the news to Linda. I held nothing back and told her everything that had happened and what was going on. She was hurt and wounded. She was angry and annoyed but at the same time she was comforting and kind. We cried together and held each other. We had a few very tense days and I wondered if she would leave me. She was even more annoyed with me that I had thought that of her. She said at one point that she had married me for better or for worse and this was one of those worse times and that she was not going to leave me. Our two daughters who were both in their last years at High School were picking up the atmosphere and were beginning to ask questions. People at church knew something was going on but nobody was saying anything. The Elders had met with me and said they wished I had spoken to them first rather than to the local network leaders. They felt that the train had left the station after they had arrived and that matters had been taken out of their hands. We all felt incredibly powerless.

A meeting was called for two weeks time in which my situation would be discussed and my future decided. Linda and I needed time to deal with our emotions and to look at our relationship because it had taken a severe blow. I wondered where God was in all this. I did not feel his love. I felt his judgement, anger and disapproval. I was looking at him through Adam's fallen eyes. I was afraid. I discussed with Linda the possibility of going away together somewhere where we could get some distance and perspective on what was happening. She agreed and we thought of Toronto.

We were able to clear our dairies, get flights booked and headed off to Toronto for a week. I did not preach the Sunday before we went, we both sat together in the congregation among the people we loved and were so much part of. I cried in the worship time as I knew things would never be the same again for us. After the meeting the old farmer who had burnt the pulpit all those years ago came to us and gave us a cheque for £500. He said he thought it would help us on the trip to Toronto. Over the next few months we would be on the receiving end of incredible love and kindness from these dear people.

The flight to Toronto was long and silent. We flew to New York rented a car and drove though up state New York and along the southern shore of Lake Eerie in a snow storm close behind a snow plough. It was Valentine's Day as we drove across the border at Niagara. We had dinner that night in the revolving restaurant in the tower overlooking the falls. We were in the Honeymoon Capital of America. It felt anything but a honeymoon to us.

Next day we parked the car at the Toronto Airport Christian Fellowship as it was then called and walked into the church. It was early afternoon. As we walked through the doors a sense of peace wafted over us. There were no meetings happening except a prayer ministry time for pastors in one of the side halls. We slipped in the back and sat down saying nothing to anyone. After some time a woman who had been sitting on the floor at the side and was one of the ministry team came over to us. She asked us if we spoke English. We nodded and then she told us that she had been watching us for some time and had seen something written over us.

"Can I share what I have seen with you?" she asked.

We agreed and she said, "I saw the word 'Restoration' written over you. I believe Father is going to bring you to a time of restoration. Does that make any sense to you?"

The tears began to pour down our faces. I didn't stop crying all week.

There was a guest ministry team there from a large church in Melbourne, Florida and we met many of them during the week. The woman who had brought that word to us was part of the team and was on the staff in the Melbourne Church. As the week progressed we both received a measure of healing and lots of prayer from these people.

One evening the preacher who was also from Melbourne preached a particularly powerful word from Zechariah 9:11-12

> *"As for you, because of the blood of my covenant with*
> *you, I will free your prisoners from the waterless pit.*
> *Return to your fortress, O prisoners of hope;*
> *even now I will restore twice as much to you."*

It was a message full of hope amidst the pain of exile and disaster. It restored some hope to us. This deeply touched me and when the ministry time began I ran to the front and very quickly was on my face sobbing and feeling God's mercy and love being poured into me. After some time as I lay face down on the ground I became aware that someone was singing and playing over me. It was the worship leader from TACF, Jeremy Sinnott, who was walking around playing his guitar and singing over people. He stopped beside me and sang "He is a merciful, merciful, merciful God."

I felt a heavy weight on my back as a hand was laid on me. It pressed heavily into me and I felt a deep peace coming over me. As I moved to look at the person who was doing this, there was no one there. I was momentarily surprised but I realised that it was the hand of God himself resting on me. He was touching me himself and was telling me I was truly forgiven and his mercy for me was ever available. One of the repeated themes of the week was, let mercy triumph over judgement. This was a week that we both desperately needed. We would need to hang onto what God had done in order to help us cope with the coming weeks and months.

On the final evening I shared a little with one of the team from Melbourne what we had been going through and as a result we were asked to share a brief testimony. We spoke of God's mercy and how I had felt his hand upon me. We were prayed for again and this time were surrounded by the ministry team from Florida. One brought a word that he felt a divine connection had been made in the spirit between us and them. In a few weeks time we would see how God was beginning to arrange our restoration and future.

On returning to the UK the next challenge was being summoned to the meeting where the local apostolic team would speak with me. I had no clear idea what had been said to everyone. Two of us drove to the meeting and I was feeling extremely anxious and fearful. Linda asked them to look after me as she was very concerned for my emotional equilibrium as I was in a very vulnerable place.

I was asked to wait outside the room for about an hour while they talked about me inside the room. Then eventually I was called in.

These were my friends, the men who I had worked closely with over the last six or seven years. They did not ask me anything. I was not asked to verify anything that they had been told. I felt I had been judged in absentia and now I was about to hear my sentence. There was some discussion about disclosure. They told me that I would have to step down from the leadership of the church. I asked about a sabbatical. This was declined. A date was fixed for a church meeting to be called when I would have an opportunity to address the church and tell them what had happened and then I would resign as the leading elder of the church. I was in deep shock. I was traumatized by this turn of events. I had not seen it coming. They told me I should leave and go home as they all needed to stay and talk some more.

I walked out to my car in the car park and completely broke down. My whole body was wracked with sobs for quite some time. Eventually I turned on the ignition and started the engine and drove out of the car park. I was driving without real thought of where I was going. In my head I could hear a voice urging me to drive faster and faster. How easy it would be to end it all. How much better it would be for Linda and the family, my friends and the church. No one would blame me, it would just be an accident. It was the easiest way out. I entered a straight section of road and pushed the pedal to the floor. I reached 70mph then 80mph. It would be for the best. It would be quick. It would be over. There was a curve coming up and I knew I was travelling much too fast to get around it safely. Suddenly I realised what was happening. I slowed down enough to get around the bend without crashing but it was a close thing. After a mile there was a lay-by where I stopped with my heart racing and again sobs wracking my body. I stayed there for about twenty minutes while I recovered. As I sat there I heard the Lord say to me,

"O afflicted city lashed by storms and not comforted,
I will build you with stones of turquoise and your
foundations with sapphires."

He came to me in the car and I began to have hope that in spite of all that was happening he would rebuild us and put in new foundations. He would restore us eventually. I returned home late that night and broke the news to Linda.

We gathered our three children the following Saturday. I sat with them and began to tell them what was going on. Why we had been so preoccupied over the last month or so but specifically I told them what I had done those years ago. I held nothing back. After a while I left them to talk it through together especially with their mother. One by one they came to me in the next little while. They hugged me and kissed me, told me they loved me and also that they forgave me. This was the most precious moment in the whole ghastly time. I realised again what a wonderful wife and children I had.

I don't know how I would have got through those days without their unconditional love and support for me.

A week later the church meeting was planned. News had leaked out that something dreadful had happened. A form of words was agreed and I was permitted to make a limited statement to the church. They said that the term "a moral failure" could be used. The logic was that it would protect the family from unnecessary pain and embarrassment. It was also felt this would stop excessive gossip. I was ready to make a fuller statement but they advised against this. I appreciated their desire to protect the family but it had the opposite effect as far as gossip was concerned. This was a small town and news was circulating everywhere by the end of the week.

It was clear that the leadership of the network felt that I had seriously compromised my ministry and that I needed a period of discipline to test, amongst other things, that I was truly repentant. It was a surprise to me that this was questioned. My point of view was I had come forward and confessed my sin in order to deal with the underlying issues. It was not as if I had been caught in the act and had been found out. There again I still had no clear idea what had been told to the national leadership.

When Linda asked for clarification on the day of the meeting about what had been actually said all she got by way of an answer was a look that said 'you poor woman you have no idea'. There was talk about denial, manipulation and control. It seemed they believed I had been operating out of this place for some time. Whatever I said would be seen as more of the same. I think I was only just beginning to grasp the full import of what this meant. I felt I was caught in a trap of words. If I questioned things I was trying to control or manipulate the situation. If I disagreed with anything obviously I was in denial. I could not win. I felt no one was willing to listen to me. We felt so alone, surrounded by friends but no-one seemed to be able to speak for us. I see now that they were also very much in a state of shock and were caught up in the whirlwind as we were and so I have sympathy for them now, but at the time I was devastated.

We walked together as a family the half mile or so to the church for the disclosure meeting. Over two hundred of the dear people of our church sat in silence as we entered. We had been told the plan was that the national leader would begin the meeting and call me forward to make my statement. Then everyone would be asked to stand while someone would lead in prayer. They told us that during the prayer the family could slip quietly away. This is what we had shared with the children and were all expecting.

I stood to make my statement, to say the words, ask for their forgiveness and I was to conclude by reading 1 Thessalonians Chapter 5 verses 12 - 25. Linda and the three children sat in the front row. As I looked at my family their faces all showed the strain of the previous days. They were still reeling from the shock that their father and husband was not the man that they had thought he was.

Alongside them were my friends, many of them fellow leaders in the church and from the wider network of which we were part. Their faces were serious and fixed on me. They knew what I was about to say. They had agreed the draft of the statement I was about to deliver. They were disappointed and sad. They were angry and shocked. They felt I had let them down, let the church down, let my family and myself down. Most of all it had been made clear to me they felt I had let God down. Several had tears in their eyes.

I stood before them all. I looked across the congregation and could feel the sense of tension that was spreading across the room. I could see bewilderment on some people's faces and anxiety in some people's eyes. After a brief pause I drew a deep breath and began to speak. I told them about my life and how I had let everyone down by having "a moral failure" some years before. How I had sinned. How I had hidden it. How I had cried out to God for forgiveness. How I had decided in recent weeks to begin to address the underlying issues. How, it was felt, as a consequence that I needed to resign as the pastor and leading elder of the church. As I finished one dear lady jumped up and said they do not want me to step down. I thanked her for her gracious response and handed the meeting back to the others.

Then to our great shock the family were asked to leave. We had been told that we would leave during the prayer but now we were simply instructed to all get up and leave the meeting. It felt as if we were all being disciplined and ejected even if that was not the intention. My actions obviously had a wide range of consequences and this was one of them that we were not expecting. Suddenly my children and my wife were being subjected to public humiliation on account of my actions and in front of everyone. They had been told this would not happen. They were let down, not only by their father, but now by the leadership of the church network in the moment when they needed the most support and sensitivity. I do not believe this was deliberate in any sense but nonetheless it happened. We walked out together all holding each others hands. At the door I foolishly turned and looked back and saw the faces of the people. At that point the emotional strain was too much and I started to collapse. I dropped my Bible and stumbled. Immediately a pair of arms were around me and were holding me up. It was my son Nick. I will never forget that moment. He was not only being a son to me but it was as if he was being the Father's arms around me, holding me at this very low point. I am so blessed to have a son like this.

Only recently have I realised what the events of those days did to our children. All of them in different ways were damaged by the experience. The pain of realisation that their father had failed and was not the man they thought he was. Their own humiliation at 'being marched out of the church meeting like naughty children in front of everyone' to quote one of them, was extremely painful. The loss of confidence in church leadership was also a deep wound. All of this has scarred them and left them wounded to some degree. They have all had to come to terms in their own way with these events and their feelings and emotions to all of these things. In writing this book I am partly writing to help them see the bigger picture of what God the Father was doing in my life and all of our lives as a family since those days. I have immense respect for each one of them and love for all three of them as I have seen them grow into mature young man and women and raise families of their own and work through their own responses. I am so proud of them.

Linda too was drawn into the whole maelstrom of those days. As my wife, she faithfully walked beside me and supported me. She slowly rebuilt her broken trust in me and stood with me in the difficult years that were ahead of us. How I wish that there had been someone who could have come alongside her in those long dark days. A few years later when Linda was having a time of healing prayer for what she had felt that night as she walked through those church doors, the Father showed her that Jesus was walking out with her and that his arms were around the whole family. He has always been with us even at the darkest of times and that night was one of the darkest.

∼

CHAPTER TWELVE

A New Day Dawns

~

Later that evening when we got home, one of the leaders who had been at the Church meeting called in to see us before he left to go back to his town. He prayed with us and wanted to reassure us that he was there for us. We really appreciated that. Of all those who had been party to the previous weeks I felt he was a man who had the needs of our whole family at heart. I felt some hope and wondered how we would move on from this point. However that night I dreamt that I was caught up in a nuclear holocaust which sums up what I felt like in many ways. It was to be the first of a number of such dreams of the coming weeks and months. In the morning there were two hand delivered letters on the door mat from church members who had written offering comfort and understanding. They wrote to express their sorrow and their grief at the turn of events. Later flowers for Linda were delivered.

Over the next few weeks we had an avalanche of letters, cards and flowers for Linda from members of the local church family. Nearly all contained expressions of love and kindness, offering forgiveness and acceptance. It was incredibly humbling. It seemed that the overwhelming response from the church was that their feelings and desires had been largely overridden and ignored. A difficult time began for the church. The man I had first shared with, was quickly put in to lead the church through this transition. He also assumed responsibility for many of the areas that had previously been mine within the wider group of churches. He began by preaching a series on Nehemiah. The implications were not lost on the people and some began to voice their concerns and opinions. I became aware that my presence in the town at this delicate time was not helpful and the last thing I wanted was to create even more unhappiness than I had already. I was told I must not go to any meetings of the church, though Linda could if she wanted to for the time being until it was decided where we should go and what they would do with us. The girls were allowed to continue attending the local church if they wanted.

The first Sunday evening after the announcement Linda and I went to the cinema. We had not done this on a Sunday night for years. It was so strange to do that. Over the next few weeks we talked about the possibility of going back to Toronto. We had heard that they had just started an R and R programme which was for Rest and Recovery. It seemed the ideal thing for me to do. We made enquires and a few days later put the idea to the local leaders. I think they were relieved that I would be away for a few weeks. Linda released me to go and agreed that she would come across to Toronto for a week in the middle of my time. In all I would be away for five weeks.

136

The church had graciously agreed to pay my salary for six months which was a great blessing to us and it gave us time to make plans for our future without too much financial pressure. So we had until the end of August. In the few weeks before I went to Toronto we were carried along by the ongoing kindness and loving support of friends in the church and some long time friends further afield. I think everyone knew that it would take time to come to any conclusions about what to do with us. In my naivety I thought we could stay on in the town and remain part of the church while we were restored and I received the counseling which had been promised. I thought there would be some sort of restoration programme put in place. I had not realised that this was being considered a disciplinary process.

One of the biggest challenges to me was, that overnight, I had changed from being a successful and sought after church leader to a former and fallen leader. This idea of being a fallen leader was new to me. I really did not know how deeply my identity was tied to what I did and how I served. Without a sphere to operate in I was not very sure what to do or indeed who I was. Who was I? This was true also for a number of others. One man, a member of the church who had come a couple of years previously with the grandiose idea that his ministry was to support the leadership, telephoned one day. He wanted to say that as his ministry was to leaders, he didn't know how he could support me now that I was no longer a leader. I thanked him as politely as I could, which was a struggle to be honest, and put the phone down. What a relief I didn't have to deal with people like that anymore.

The departure for Toronto came very quickly and I took a flight to Canada. I found it very hard to leave Linda as I felt that our relationship was still fragile and strained. She assured me that it would be okay. She wanted to stay at home and be with the girls, the oldest of whom was in her final year of High School. On arriving at Toronto Airport Christian Fellowship (TACF) I was met by the programme coordinator and introduced to my hosts for the next five weeks. They were a lovely Dutch couple in their mid sixties who had a beautiful house in the country, north of the city. It would be the perfect place to bury myself for a while and spend time with God.

They had an extensive video library including many of recent speakers at the church. So I was well set up to work on my stuff, or rather let God work on my stuff. There was another couple there who were also on the same programme. Life quickly settled into a rhythm. Each day began with a scrumptious breakfast when we would chat together and I noticed that Henry and Beth began to probe and make suggestions on what to read or watch. In the mornings I spent time reading and the book that was first on my list was Gordon MacDonald's classic, 'Rebuilding Your Broken World.' I had started keeping a journal about two months before so that was another daily activity. I would fix my own lunch and then head off to the Church where there were various activities happening each day such as soaking, prophetic prayer times and leaders' meetings. This last one gave me the most problem because I did not feel I qualified for these sessions any more. Henry advised me to attend everything. Each evening there were renewal meetings and I went to all of them and took every opportunity to get prayed for.

The first two weeks passed quite slowly and I spent a lot of time on my own not really talking to anyone. This was pre email, so communicating with Linda was hard. We regularly spoke on the phone. There were times when we both were feeling very low and missing each other and we looked forward to being together again.

By the time Linda arrived Henry and Beth were fully apprised of our situation and had made themselves available to us if we wanted it.

We had a very rich and enjoyable week together in Toronto and even managed to drive to the hinterland of lakes and hills in the area of Ontario north of the city. We attended as many meetings as we could at the church but above all else we spent time together and with Henry and Beth and their friend Faye. They took us through a time of deep ministry in the area of our relationship and the wounds that we had suffered because of my brokeness. They prayed through in detail the significant moments in my life where the enemy had attacked me and I had fallen into sinful behaviour. It was a systematic yet Spirit led approach. I asked for and received forgiveness. I held nothing back from Linda. Areas where I had not opened my heart to her for fear of rejection I now opened and she lovingly and purposefully forgave me and loved me. We both received great healing in that week. We are so glad that God gave us these wonderful people to help us through this time. Our relationship began to be restored and was placed on a new level of openness and commitment.

This was God beginning to deal with my stuff and I was happy about that. The process of getting to this place was extremely painful but worth it as healing flowed. We both felt that he had provided us with a safe place among people who were not judging us or who were not angry with me. This was to be the first of a number of places God would take us to in order to remove the roots from which my stuff had been drawing its life. I did not have any idea that he would be still doing this today fifteen years later. I have learned that the journey he has me on would ultimately bring me to a place of knowing him as my loving Father. At this point I felt it was a deep work of the Spirit and that was a place that I was familiar with and open to. God started at a place where I felt safe and gradually from there was taking me into a deeper walk with him. Even though Toronto Airport Christian Fellowship's mission statement was 'To walk in his love and give it away', it never really crossed my mind who "his "was. I just assumed that this was the Lord. I had not seen him as Father even though it was called the Father's blessing. I did not consciously connect with the Father as it was more about the Holy Spirit in my mind and experience. That was what I was open to and that was where he was meeting me. Now I know that this is how the Father comes to us. He wants us to know him at heart level and experience him as a Father but for many of us we cannot go there until those wounded areas that get in the way are healed. He takes us from where we are to where he is and it does not matter to him how long it takes.

I learned this one day recently when I had the opportunity to meet William P. Young, known as Paul, the author of the book called The Shack. Talking with Paul we discussed his presentation of God the Father as Papa, a black American woman. There has been some controversy about the way Paul Young characterizes 'God' in this way. The idea that God would appear to Mack, the main human character of the book as a black woman is because in the early part of the story he could not see God as a Father. However it needs to be remembered that this is a work of fiction in the genre of Pilgrim's Progress. It was only later as Mack's heart begins to be healed and he could see God as a Father that Papa appears to him as a man. In C. Baxter Kruger's book The Shack Revisted, Kruger addresses this issue.

Kruger is exploring the way Jesus speaks to the broken and outcasts in Luke chapter 15 through the three parables about the lost sheep, the lost coin and the parable known as the Prodigal son. Kruger says, "Jesus was telling them that they were accepted and loved by his Father just like this Jewish patriarch loved his broken son. Like the shepherd, Jesus' Abba has come after his lost sheep. Like the woman, Jesus' Papa has scoured the house of his universe to find his lost coin. And like this Jewish father, Jesus' Abba has embraced and kissed us in our shame, and commanded a feast in his joy. So what's the real difference between an African-American woman embracing a broken, angry white man, and a Jewish father embracing his wayward son? Both are stunning pictures of the truth."

Kruger continues and says, "Paul Young is not saying that God is a black woman, any more than Jesus is saying that God is a Jewish patriarch. But both are using a shocking story to help us know the real truth about Jesus' Father, and the truth about who we are." (The Shack Revisited p25)

When Linda returned to the UK, I had two weeks left and I wondered what God had in store for me next. Back in February we had connected with the ministry team that came from a church in Melbourne, Florida. They had left an open invitation to go and visit anytime. I made contact and asked if I could visit for a weekend. They replied that I was more than welcome to come but make it a long weekend and share in the leaders meetings and various things that were planned. Our contact was Sandy, the woman who had brought the word to us about Restoration. She arranged accommodation for me in the home of one of the associate pastors, a recently widowed man in his mid 60s.

I flew from Toronto to Tampa, rented a car and drove to Melbourne. On the drive I contemplated what I would say because

I imagined the question "So why have you come to Florida?" might legitimately be asked. I carefully constructed a brief and clinically tidy answer which went along the lines of. "I am a former pastor who has had a fall as a result of a moral failure and I am in recovery in Toronto and have come to visit and just see what God is doing here." It was very neat and tidy.

Sure enough, not long after had I met my host he asked me the question and I trotted out my answer. We were sitting outside John's house by his swimming pool eating a plate of nachos and salsa covered with melted cheese. John had been widowed about eighteen months previously. He was a tall silver haired man, tanned by the Florida sun and also due in part to his Cherokee Indian heritage. He looked more like a man in his early fifties than his mid sixties. He was incredibly relaxed and at ease. After I gave my little speech he looked at me with a look that I found quite disarming and said. "Hmm, so what do you know about our church?" It was an odd question because I knew absolutely nothing other than they had been, like so many around the world, profoundly affected by the move which had begun in Toronto.

John began to tell me that the church was founded by the well known author, Jamie Buckingham. Jamie had come there on the back of a moral failure of his own and was being restored to ministry by God. As part of that he had settled in Melbourne and planted a church. Into the fabric of the church he had built a culture of restoration of those who had fallen. Indeed over half of the current staff had been through a similar experience including the man sitting opposite me. He briefly shared his story of how he had come there with his wife after a failure which had taken place in a church where he was senior Pastor in New England about ten years previously. He looked at me again with the look that has since become so familiar to me and said. "Well, son, I think Father has set you up, don't you! Would you like to tell me the real story now?"

Needless to say I burst into tears. Back in February, when we had gone so wounded and broken to Toronto, unbeknown to us Father was already putting the plan together to bring me to Melbourne and to meet this wonderful man of God who would in many ways oversee the next phase of our journey.

Two hours later I was done. My story had all been poured out I had held nothing back. John prayed for me, for Linda and the children, he prayed a prayer full of hope, full of anticipation for what God was going to do. John has a son my age but from that day I felt in some way I was like a son to him and he was like a father to me. It was something that I had never felt before. Much of my pain had come from looking for love and affection from a father and not receiving it or worse, it becoming sexualised. This has never been my experience with John. He and his second wife Susan remain firm friends to this day. Recently we walked on the same beach in Florida where we have so often walked and I told him that I have always considered him to be like a father to me. He just gave me one of those looks.

Throughout the week in Melbourne we would sit by the pool in the warm balmy evenings of southern Florida in the spring. Every evening John slowly and lovingly encouraged me to unpack more of my stuff. It is as if he was reviewing all that we had worked through in Toronto. We prayed each night. He addressed the issue of self loathing that I felt and the shame that I felt towards myself. He also began to prepare me for going back to the UK which I was due to do in less than a week. Already fear was beginning to build up in my heart about the future and what we would do. I would need to get a job and in spite of all the good things we had received in the recent weeks this had all happened in North America and we would be in the UK, far away from these new friends.

When I left Florida I knew that we would go back there. I very much wanted to go there. It was as if I wanted to run away to somewhere warm, where I was not known and where I could hide. We have been back to Florida numerous times and John and Susan have come to our home many times. We tried to move there and even bought a house there but we never lived in it. It was just to be a place of refreshment and relaxation that God provided for us. The relationship with John and Susan was not limited to Florida.

On returning to Toronto for the final few days my anxiety levels began to rise about my return to the UK. Two nights before leaving I was at the church for one of the renewal meetings and bumped into two familiar faces. It was a couple from the church of the man who had orchestrated the events leading up to my resignation. My stomach was gripped by fear and twisted inside. I felt as if I was going to pass out as panic swept through me. We spoke briefly and I fled. This did not bode well for my return to the UK. I was immensely grateful for all that God had done during my R & R time in Toronto at the Airport Christian Fellowship. However I was uncertain what would await me on my return.

~

CHAPTER THIRTEEN

Dark Days

~

On returning to Norfolk I felt a mixture of thankfulness for all that God had done in us both while in Toronto but also a sense of foreboding. It was very good to be back with the family but at the same time I learnt that Linda had been relieved of all responsibility for anything at the church. Indeed the new leader had suggested that she should no longer meet with people on an informal basis as her obvious distress was too much for people to cope with. I was angry about this. What had she done? Who should she turn to for support and encouragement? I felt she was becoming marginalised on my account. I found myself becoming increasingly angry about things. Sadly much of the peace and relief I had experienced in Toronto and Florida dissipated far more quickly than I had hoped.

About a week after my return we received a letter from the person who had been overseeing my situation telling us it had been decided that for our good we must move to another town and completely different area with immediate effect. It was felt it was not helpful for us to stay in Norfolk and that the leaders of another church in that town would take on responsibility for us. This was a bombshell when it arrived. It was not what I was expecting and it seemed to completely overlook the fact that Linda had a full time job which was a key part of our income at that time. Also both our girls were in the last two years of the High School. I foolishly reacted and wrote comments to this effect in the margin of the letter and photocopied it for each of the elders at the church. My comments were full of my angry reaction so it was really no surprise that it was not well received. This was not the wisest move. It had a very negative reception locally and from the national team which is not at all surprising. Sadly it had the effect of losing the point I was making about the needs of the family and more focused on my anger and my anxiety.

Added to this there were a growing number of people in the local church who were publicly and vocally expressing their concern about our situation and how it had been handled. It did not help that a number of these people had come to see us to encourage us. It became apparent that our every move was being watched and monitored by others. Things I was supposed to be saying or not saying were being reported and it was becoming very difficult for us. I had been allowed to attend the church on one or two occasions but that was no longer permitted. I was feeling very rejected and abandoned by my former group of friends who were mostly elders in the local group of churches. One day I was out walking with one of them and he confided in me that my mistake was to admit that I had a problem. Why hadn't I just kept my mouth shut? I said that everyone had issues and surely it should be a good thing for elders to deal with their stuff. I know there was a great sense of irony in my voice because I personally was questioning that logic. This colleague of mine stopped in his tracks and said to me,

"Do you think any of us want to deal with our stuff and go through what you are going through?"

The tragedy of this statement has stayed with me for many years.

When the Apostle John wrote his first letter, in chapter 1 he addresses this issue. He says in verse 7,

> *"if we walk in the light, as he is in the light, we have fellowship with one another, and the blood of Jesus, his Son, purifies us from all sin."*

The Apostle Paul in Ephesians, chapter 5 verse 7 says,

> *"For you were once in darkness, but now you are light in the Lord. Walk as children of light"*

Both John and Paul envisioned a community of people who were learning to walk as Jesus walked, in the love of God the Father and walking in relationship with each other in love. Walking in the light implies an openness between each other that recognizes our weaknesses, our need for forgiveness and acceptance of one another. It does not condone sinful action and activity but seeks to lovingly restore and help one another.

This attitude of heart has been very clearly and helpfully written about in Danny Silk's book "Culture of Honor". When we value and honour each other, walking in the light brings freedom and willingness to address our issues. If we feel that we are going to be exposed and judged, that we are going to be rejected and publicly shamed, then there is not a culture of honour and it promotes a desire to hide our stuff and issues. This is the opposite of what is needed when someone falls.

Paul writing to the Galatians in chapter 6 address this with the early church.

> *"Brothers, if someone is caught in any sin, you who are spiritual should restore such a one in a spirit of gentleness; each one looking to yourself, so that you too will not be tempted. Carry one another's burdens, and in this way you will fulfill the law of Christ. For if anyone thinks he is something when he is nothing, he deceives himself. Each one should test his own actions. Then he can take pride in himself, without comparing himself to somebody else, for each one should carry his own load."*

In the midst of the trauma of failure, Paul and John are encouraging a loving supportive, community of brothers and sisters, walking in the light, who carry each others burdens when they stumble and fall and are not able to carry their own load. The last thing that they envisioned was a culture where people are afraid to bring their issues to the light. Instead they encouraged a redemptive community of love.

In 'Culture of Honor', Danny Silk address the very real issues that arise when leaders sin and fail. In particular he explores how they are dealt with by others in leadership. Chapter 4 of his book explores the process of restoration that is needed in these situations. I would strongly recommend reading the whole book since it offers such a tangible and workable alternative. Danny Silk asks what is the true nature of restoration? He says that an old meaning of the word "restoration" was to find someone with a royal bloodline who had been removed from the throne and then restore the person to the throne - to a position of honour. Scholars of British history will recall the restoration of King Charles II to the throne in 1660.

However putting a monarch back in his or her place of authority is rarely what the process that is called "restoration" looks like when dealing with leaders in the church who have broken the rules. Silk goes on to say that most fallen leaders leave their churches or denominations and go and find a "fresh start" which means that they find a group of people who are not afraid of them breaking the rules again. I completely understand this line of thought as this is how these things unfolded for us. This was my experience exactly. Sadly at the time I was going through this we were unaware of any alternative.

One of the key issues in these situations is the repentance of the individual who has committed some sort of misdemeanor. The Bethel Church in Redding, California where Danny Silk is based seeks to bring confrontation to the individual in order to encourage genuine heartfelt repentance that recognizes the seriousness of the situation and demonstrates a willingness to enter into a season of change and healing to get to the root issue.

Danny Silk continues by saying that when God restores those who have repented, his process of restoration looks like reestablishing a royal family member in his or her place of rulership and honor. The restored believer can say, "I *now feel accepted as a son of God again.*" Silk sees the restoration for the believer as always restoration of relationship because restoration is defined by the cross and restoration to relationship is what the cross did. At this point in my story I barely had any idea what it meant to be a son of God in reality. This realisation was to come much later in my journey. However I understand the point being made.

Contacts with these work colleagues became less and it became clear that I was in trouble and they really wanted me out of the area. Some did understand the difficulty over jobs for us both and what to do about the girls. If I had felt that there was a real heart behind the proposed move I would have seriously gone to Bedford. I received a written response to my concerns that suggested the girls should lodge with somebody in the church in Norfolk. Again I was angry. In the middle of all that they had gone through with their father and the associated shame and embarrassment that they must have felt we were now being told to leave our daughters and break up our family. This was not an option any of us were prepared to consider. I said I could not go and asked for an alternative to be considered.

What we lacked at this crucial and traumatic time was an advocate who could speak on our behalf or a team of trusted people who would regularly meet with us and help us through this period. We felt so alone. Those who had offered us support began to feel that they were being viewed with suspicion by the leadership. Since then I have researched various churches and groups that have sought to restore fallen leaders. One of the essential component parts that they all seem to say is an important part of the process is a restoration team that acts as an advocate. This needs to be put in place within a very short space of time after the fall has been disclosed. We have discovered this in hindsight. However we were not in that place and we felt very much alone. In the midst of all this we received a fax from Florida. It was from John. "Thinking of you and praying for you right now" is what it said. How I wished I had someone like John who was nearby to calm me down, to stop me over reacting and to help me deal with my anger.

For quite sometime Linda had done a large amount of grief

counseling especially during our time in Norfolk. As we talked it became apparent that I was going through a grief process. The loss for me was my identity as much as anything else. Many people when made redundant from their jobs experience similar reactions. After the initial shock and numbness, and the denial that the loss was not really as serious as it appeared there comes the stage of anger. I was in this stage right now. I was angry at myself, at God at times but especially at the men who I thought had been friends. Now I felt they had betrayed me. The language says it all really. I was in a very bad place indeed. I was experiencing feelings that I did not know I had.

I was caught unconsciously in a triangle of reactions. Sometimes I felt I had perpetrated a great crime. I needed a rescuer and then I became a victim. At times I saw others as the perpetrators against me and I and my family were now the victims. I had no understanding of this at the time or how to break out of this dramatic and vicious triangle which left all of us as losers.

At one stage I felt I was nearing a complete emotional breakdown. I certainly had slipped into a time of depression. The true magnitude of my loss was overwhelming me. Everything that I had wanted to be and achieve had been removed in humiliation almost overnight. It was my own fault. I had many deep rooted ungodly beliefs that were now drawing heavily on the lies that the devil and his cronies had whispered. Lies that said I was a failure. I was a disappointment. I was alone. I was abandoned. I was untrustworthy. During those days it seemed I was barely hanging on to my sanity. I could not find God in this time. I could not read my Bible. I could not pray. I would walk my dog, Bilbo, for hours every day on the lonely heaths of Norfolk, crying and sometimes shouting. Poor old Bilbo he just looked at me and would, from time to time, come and sit at my feet with his head on my knee giving me one of his looks. I felt God comforting me through my dog! I wonder what the critics of The Shack would make of that!

Then quite suddenly in the midst of all this time of pain and uncertainty Linda's father died, totally unexpectedly. Linda had been doing so well and was a huge support in many ways keeping us all together. The very week her father died we had a letter from the church saying that it had been decided, by the regional oversight, that we were no longer welcome at the local church. The girls could continue to attend if they so wished but we could not. This was a heavy blow most especially for Linda. When she need the added support of friends in the church as she struggled with the loss of her beloved father she was denied that access. We were permitted to attend a church in the nearby city. This was cold comfort.

These were dark days indeed. I think these friends really didn't know what to do with us and it didn't help that I was so angry and upset. There are always two sides to every broken relationship and I know it was not easy for them either. It saddens me to this day that I have no real relationship with some of these men who once had been such close friends. It is said that time heals. No, it doesn't! Only the Father can heal our hearts and bring genuine restoration and reconciliation between people. I look forward to the time when one day we can look into each others eyes and face the pain of the past and give and receive forgiveness and be reconciled to one another. Perhaps this is a chapter that will be written one day and I'll have to rewrite some of this book.

During the summer I began to recover slightly. I did not feel there was much else that could happen to make matters worse so I began to have a little more hope. When I said that we could not move at that time and we were permitted to attend a church in the city nearby it was as if the wider leadership washed their hands of us. Later on I discovered that was effectively what had happened. It was being said we had refused to follow the restoration process that had been put in place. After that it was clear there was nothing more that they would do. We were viewed to be in rebellion and were no longer their responsibility. We started attending the church that had been designated to take us but I felt so awkward and conspicuous. I felt like the elephant in the room who everyone knew was there but no one talked about. Each meeting we attended was so painful that little by little we stopped attending. As August came I knew that my pay would stop and I wondered what we would do, how we would manage, what job I could do. I felt very scared and wondered where on earth was God in all this. Was this what dealing with my stuff was all about? If so, I didn't much like it and I didn't like God much either. At times I felt he had completely abandoned us. These were very dark days.

~

CHAPTER FOURTEEN

More Light

~

We had been talking about what I could do for a job and we saw in a national paper that there was a nationwide shortage of Religious Education teachers in High Schools. They were recruiting theology graduates for the coming term. That is what I was! I applied and was accepted in the space of about three weeks. I even managed to secure a grant towards my fees and tuition. It was one of the last years that they did that. So from September I started training as an R.E. Teacher. Another new chapter was about to begin.

Training to be a Religious Education teacher was a real eye opener to a part of British life and particularly education that I had been very isolated from. I enrolled at the University of Greenwich in south east London to study for a Post Graduate Certificate in Education. It was a year's course of study most of which would be based in a High School somewhere, learning on the job alongside a qualified R.E. Teacher. The first few weeks however we were based at the University in London.

I joined a group of eighteen people who were on this course.

What a motley group of odd balls we were! It is very alarming that many young people's exposure to any form of religious information, knowledge and instruction would come from people who are on the far end of the religious crack pot scale. Only three could be remotely described as Christian, not that this was the criteria required by the teaching authorities. The subject was to be taught in an impartial way and a faith stance was not required so anyone with a degree in theology, religious studies or anything vaguely religious was acceptable.

Our lecturer met us on the first day of the course and presented us with three weeks worth of research and private study into the six major world religions that form the National Curriculum for R.E. He then said he would be away for three weeks on a spiritual retreat where he hoped to discover his true self. He was heading off to a Greek Island where he said, amongst other things, he would roll naked in the morning dew on the grass and commune with his inner man. Three weeks later he returned duly invigorated and announced that in future we should address him as 'Eagle' as this was who he discovered he really was. It was going to be an interesting year. What amazed me most was how seriously most of the group listened to him and marveled at how authentically spiritual they though he was. I just wanted to giggle.

The year included a placement in a High School for the major part of a school term. I was able to secure a position in a small town in Norfolk very near to our home which made life a lot easier. At the end of that year I was offered a permanent position at the same school as the only R.E. teacher in the school and was therefore head of department. This was a wonderful provision. I stayed at the school for a full year.

In many ways it was a great challenge teaching virtually the entire school Religious Education. British law requires all students to have one hour a week religious education right up to the age of 16. This is not popular with the vast majority who consider the subject irrelevant and boring. The R.E. teacher is considered the dullest teacher in the school, so this was a great challenge to me. We were not allowed in any way to share our own convictions lest we be guilty of indoctrinating the children. Equally we had to teach impartially all the six major world religions. I remember well one lad in year 10 complaining in his broad Norfolk accent the he did not see any point studying, "about them Islams, cus we hint got none in Narfolk. Besides I is gonna work wiv my Dad on his chicken farm." This was obviously pre 9/11 and Al Qaeda. I did my best and by the end of the year was encouraged how many of the children decided that studying R.E. was not as bad as they had thought it would be.

However my heart was not really in this and I felt it was just a means to an end. If nothing else it gave me time to begin to recover and to think about the future. I thought that a teaching qualification would be useful if we ever decided to perhaps work overseas somewhere. We had never lost sight of the call to the nations. Throughout the training year and the first year while I acquired qualified teacher status we were very much on our own. Nothing appeared to officially be in place as far as any sense of being restored was concerned nor support to deal with any of the underlying issues, so we just carried on with our lives. We were very lonely and I felt I was 'persona non grata.' We deliberately tried to avoid getting involved in any of the struggles that were going on in our former church. I was very saddened to hear that a significant number of people had left the church, some fell away completely while others just started attending other congregations. Former staff members whom I had brought on were laid off. I felt very responsible for this. It added to my sense of failure and disappointment.

We went over to Florida each year to stay with John and his new wife, Susan. At Easter 1997 we also went to Toronto staying with Henry and Beth again, and taking our oldest daughter, Sanna, with us. She then stayed on for a youth conference. We then went down to Florida taking with us Chrissie and a friend of hers. This is when John met Linda for the first time.

Later that year we went again for Christmas with Chrissie who was enjoying the new connections in Florida. Our other daughter, Sanna went off to South Africa for several weeks to stay with new friends she had made in Cape Town while there on an evangelism team. That Christmas we were on three different continents with our son, Nick, being back in the UK. It was the shape of things to come.

At the end of my first year teaching I decided to resign because I really did not want to be a full time teacher. It had given us breathing space as we began to rebuild our lives. Our church situation was frustrating and finally we decided to leave, along with the network of churches it was linked to and which we had been part of for nearly ten years. We joined a new church that had recently started up nearby in the city and were welcomed warmly by people who wanted to include us. This was new and a huge relief. The leadership expressed concern for us and wanted to do everything they could to rehabilitate us back into a healthier place. We were overwhelmed by their kindness and openness to us. We cried a number of times in those early weeks as we sat in the Sunday meetings simply from the sheer relief and of the feeling that we were welcome.

Some months later the leaders of the new church we were attending wrote a letter to the national leader of the network that had started the disciplinary process. This letter was supported by John from Florida who came over for a visit and another friend who had been seeing me regularly all through my teacher training year. He and his wife were friends from Berkhamsted days and had been another of those who had come alongside us in our time of need. The letter was jointly signed and told of where we were at spiritually and emotionally and asked if they would consider releasing us to function again in our gifting and to allow us to move on. What we felt was that we were stuck emotionally and bound by the situation. I had a strong sense of being bound by what I perceived as an apostolic ruling. Now what these friends and leaders were trying to get for us was a sense of closure and release. The response they received, whilst polite, made it very clear that in his view we had withdrawn ourselves from the process and we were no longer his responsibility. What we did and where we went was of no concern of his. He declined to meet them or us to enable a closure to happen. This was again disappointing. To this day I have never felt that it was finished or we were released by them. When we have met people I knew from those days there has been a surprising openness towards us and on a number of occasions sadness expressed by them over the way our situation was conducted. I know there is still unfinished business to do in this area of my heart.

After I resigned my teaching post at School, both girls left home in order to start their university courses at opposite ends of the country. Linda and I decided to take ourselves off to Melbourne Florida for a month. We stayed in a small cabin on the property owned by the widow of Jamie Buckingham who had been a prolific Christian writer in the 1980s and 1990s and we waited to see what might happen. A job opportunity emerged at the church in Melbourne and I seriously considered applying. I so much wanted to be back in ministry. I think on reflection that I was not in anyway ready for that. It was as if I wanted to regain some sort of status or regain my identity as a pastor or leader. I was chasing ministry because it would me give me a sense of acceptance and identity. This was not what God had planned for me at that particular time or any time.

During one of these visits to Florida we met a friend of John's who was from the Airport Church in Toronto, Guy Chevreau. He had written amongst other things a historical perspective of all the events that had gone on in Toronto during the height of the Renewal as it was then being called. We talked together and he told us about a mission trip he was taking to a Christian Drug rehabilitation ministry in Spain called Betel. He invited me to join him later in the year. On returning from Florida I went with friends to a week long conference being run by Leanne Payne. She is the author of a number of books on issues of brokenness including "Crisis in Masculinity" which I had read. The conference was a very important part of my learning to understand something of the roots of my pain and deeper issues. Yet again it was a time for healing.

I did some part time supply teaching and some voluntary work at a Christian charity that worked with people who had drug and alcohol problems called the Matthew Project which was based in Norwich. This was run by a friend who had consistently supported us over the time since my fall. He had been a great encouragement to us and his welcoming us to the Matthew Project was part of that. I started working part time then eventually I ended up working full time at the Project. Through a contact at the Matthew Project I went to Mombassa, Kenya to teach Church History at an Anglican theological college for two weeks. Various opportunities began to open up and I felt that on one level we were beginning to recover. On one of the visits to Florida we were at a large praise gathering and we found ourselves singing the song "You turned my mourning to dancing again, you lifted my sorrow." We looked at each other and realised we were both singing and smiling. This was the first time in a very long time that we remotely felt like that.

As our daughters progressed through their University courses we saw that it was going to be very expensive to pay for their housing after their first year in Halls of Residence. We helped both of them to move into their rooms with all their belongings in the respective universities. While we were doing this we took the opportunity to look at the price of property in their areas to see if there was a way to buy a house for them to live in along with other students for the coming year. Newcastle and London were very expensive and the properties we saw, very run down so this was not a financial option. We came back to Norfolk and looked into properties close to the University in Norwich. After some time we discovered that by remortgaging our own house we would have enough money to buy an ex council house in the city. This we did and after a small amount of internal remodeling we rented it out to students. It worked amazingly well and provided much needed income to supplement the girls' accommodation in their student rentals. The following year we reworked the whole mortgage deal and ended up buying three more houses, which we rented out to students.

My friend John in Florida started to call me the Rental Baron! A new identity perhaps. Soon after the end of our ministry in Norfolk in the middle of all the pain and angst I vowed I would never again be beholden to Christians for my income. I vowed that I would manage my own income and be independent. This was classic orphan like reaction to the pain of those circumstances. We finally made the decision to move out of our house and into the city. So rather than sell we rented the house out and we moved into a rental property. During that time our older daughter got married to a great guy she had met while doing a year of training and evangelism before going to university. The wedding was to be held in Bedford at the church where we were meant to have moved to about three years before. It was a lovely day and it was the opportunity to meet a number of people face to face. Whilst I found it a challenge they were nothing but warm and friendly.

The mission trip with Guy Chevreau to Spain and Portugal was excellent and very demanding. I asked, if he went again, would be possible for Linda and me to join him. I wanted her to experience these times together. He willingly agreed. So next time Guy went we both flew to Madrid to join his team. We had been told to travel light as there would be eight of us in a van and not much room for luggage. We anticipated from the previous experience that the men would go to a men's house and the women to a girl's house. We had both prepared ourselves to be sharing a dorm with ex prostitutes in Linda's case and ex addicts and drug dealers in my case. In fact we stayed together in a couple's house along with other married team members.

On arrival in Madrid airport we were told that we would be met by someone from Betel. We stood in the arrivals hall at Madrid Airport waiting. There was no sign of anyone from Betel to meet us. After about an hour we noticed another couple standing looking around, who also appeared to be travelling light. We looked at each other and eventually made eye contact and wandered over. We enquired if they were by any chance waiting for someone from Betel. They laughed and said they were. This was Dennis and Melanie Morgan-Dohner from the USA. We had just met the next couple who would help us on our journey and whose ministry to us would bring a huge amount of light and insight into the pain that was still so raw and just below the surface.

During the week travelling around Spain with Guy and the team we visited all manner of different places were Betel was at work. It was a tremendous story of hope and healing that we were seeing. The team was an interesting group of Americans, Brits and Canadians. Dennis and Mel were typically loud Americans full of laughter and joy. At times they were irritatingly happy in my somewhat glum opinion. Mel would often regale us with what she called healing stories. They were ex Vineyard Pastors and founders of a ministry called Big God Ministries, started after Dennis had been overwhelmed by the Holy Spirit in Toronto. It seemed that whenever anyone mentioned that God was a big God, Dennis would experience a loud manifestation of the Spirit as he would exclaim, "BIG GOD!" much to the amusement to everyone in ear shot.

They both had experienced significant personal physical healing in the years since the start of the Toronto Outpouring. Dennis had been healed from heart disease and Mel from cancer. Their daughters too had been healed from severe dyslexia, allergies and asthma. Since these experiences they began to travel and share their stories in many countries. They believed in the reality of physical healing and healing of the wounds that are buried in our hearts. They would regularly ask the Holy Spirit to shine his light into the dark places and would encourage people to work with what the Holy Spirit was doing. It was interesting seeing them at work. On the long journeys in the minibus across Spain occasionally "people's stuff would come up" as Mel would say. It happens when you cram people together in a confined, uncomfortable space for hours on end. There was one couple there that seemed to find the whole team thing very hard and there would be occasional outbursts of frustration expressed. Mel would smile and say sweetly, "There's healing for that!" Then perhaps add, "You don't have to live with that pain or that lie."

When we returned to the UK we kept in touch with the Morgan-Dohners or the MDs as we affectionately called them. We heard that they would be visiting the UK and we arranged to meet them at a conference in Croydon at the eccentrically named church, Folly's End.

We enjoyed meeting them again and invited them to visit us any time in Norfolk. We had moved out into the countryside by this time and had rented a very beautiful and recently renovated farm house. It was called Church Farm House. We lived there for three years and had a very happy time playing the country gentleman in our acre and a half of garden. The house was big enough for a number to stay and we had a several weekend house parties. Regulars at these gatherings were the MDs. Dennis and Mel would come to us when they had a few down days and we gave them their own room and space to just be themselves when not ministering.

We were getting to know them very well and had talked about their approach to healing of the heart which they called "More Light". They introduced us to the idea that throughout our lives and in particular from our earliest days we had been lied to by the devil. They showed us passages such as John 8 where Jesus describes the devil as the father of lies. We began to see how we have been lied to and how these lies have become a source of our life rather than the truth that we hear from God. In John 8 Jesus says,

"You shall know the truth and the truth will set you free."

Mel and Dennis taught that when a lie is exposed and we see how we have believed that lie then we can repent of that wrong belief and ask for forgiveness from God. They asked the Holy Spirit to shine his light on our hearts to see when this lie was planted and if there are other things attached to that lie that might have added to our ungodly beliefs.

These lies are so often rooted in real life events that have happened in our pasts some of which have long been buried. Often the memory is still painful as the devil has used these events to torment us for many years. After the Holy Spirit has uncovered stuff and the lies come to the light there is a greater freedom to repent. Finally they asked the Holy Spirit to show what was really happening at that time when we were lied to. They asked the Holy Spirit to reveal where Jesus was when the lie was being sown. When people sensed they had seen Jesus in the memory they were encouraged to ask him what the truth was and how he saw the situation. Often this in itself brought out all manner of ungodly beliefs about Jesus and exposed all manner of things that were hidden and needed to come to the light. They always asked people to speak to him and check that it was Jesus that they are speaking to before engaging in any conversation. There then usually followed a dialogue in which Jesus spoke life giving truth to the person receiving ministry. The results of this time and time again were incredible freedom for people. So many began to really discover who they really were in Christ rather than who they thought they were having believed all manner of satanic lies for so long.

I had read about healing of the memories and I had considerable reservations about some aspects of so called Inner Healing. As I listened and watched them minister there were a number of key differences that I found particularly helpful. First of all the whole process was led by Holy Spirit, they acted as facilitators who watch what was happening. They did not make directive suggestions or tell people what they thought. They helped people speak to and listen to the voice of Jesus for themselves. When a memory emerged they encouraged people to stay with the memory and to ask the Jesus questions in order to get clarity. When anything unclear was said they would consistently encourage people to ask him to clarify what he was saying. The other significant difference was before any one engaged in a dialogue with the one they thought was Jesus, the MDs got people to ask a simple question, "Who are you?" They then asked what answer was given. In many cases there were all sorts of strange voices that people had been listening to in their hearts. They would not continue until the reply came "I am Jesus." Sometimes people would hear things like "I am the one you have always prayed to," or "I am your friend," or "I'm the one who knows you best." Whenever voices like this were heard they encouraged people to send them away.

It surprised me how so many people were listening to demons masquerading as angels of light, wolves in sheep's clothing and even figments of their own imaginations. Most doubted that they would ever hear the voice of God but were quite happy to listen to other voices. One individual would not ask, "Who are you?" when he saw someone he said was Jesus. He was convinced he was talking to Jesus because he could see him in the memory wearing a long, blue and white robe and holding his fingers up in the form of a religious blessing. Eventually he asked 'who are you?' and the reply he received shook him deeply. It said, "I am Catholic Religion." He immediately told it to go away and suddenly saw another figure who after being asked, "Who are you? He heard him say, "I am Jesus." The man had the most amazing life changing conversation that released him from huge amounts of guilt, shame and wrong beliefs.

One other aspect of the prayer ministry that impressed me was that there was no suggestion that the memories were changed by this experience. What changed was the perception of the memory when they saw that Jesus was with them in their darkest moments. Very often at the end of a session, which typically did not last for more than two hours, people were asked to think about the painful memory again to see if there was still pain attached to it. Invariably the person was free from pain and in possession of revelatory truth that they had heard in their hearts, directly from Jesus. The MDs had said very little throughout but had just listened in and helped occasionally when people got stuck. It was remarkably uncomplicated and had dramatic results by way of healing.

Mel had said to me on one occasion that they had been qualified Christian counsellors seeing people, sometimes for numerous sessions, with very little change occurring. Since they had started to develop and use the More Light approach they were seeing many people experience very real and lasting healing and they were not needing to come back time and again for more sessions.

One day as we sat with the Mel and Dennis in Church Farm House, enjoying the view over the beautiful North Norfolk countryside I made a comment something like.

"You know, deep inside when something happens I have always felt I am a disappointment and will let people down."

Not surprisingly Mel put down her book, looked me in the eyes and said.

"Trevor, there is healing for that. Do you want to go there now?"

Together we asked the Holy Spirit to come and show me when this sense of disappointment began. It was suggested that I close my eyes and wait and to not try to think up things. I was asked to speak out aloud anything that came to mind however irrelevant it might seem. Almost immediately I remembered the story that my aunts had told me when I was a young boy of how my father was disappointed when I was born and that I was not the hoped for girl. As we began to explore this memory I thought about how that made me feel when I was a young boy hearing that story. Together we asked the Spirit to show me if there was a lie attached to this in any way. I began to realise that the devil had lied to me because what I believed was that I was a disappointment. It was not just that my parents had been disappointed. They led me to see that by agreeing with the lie and believing it was true, I was effectively giving the devil permission to continually repeat his accusation every time something happened that was disappointing. It became clear that I needed to hear the truth to break the power of this lie and be set free of the continual effect it was having on me.

We asked the Spirit to show me when the devil implanted the lie in my life. Immediately I had a strange picture form in my mind that I knew was being put there by the Spirit. It was not a memory because what I saw was my mother about to give birth to me. In that moment, I knew that it was the day I was born that the devil had lied to me and told me I was not welcome because I was not a girl and that I was therefore a disappointment and would always be a disappointment and I would never be what people had hoped I would be. As a baby this was not anything I was aware of at a conscious level but in my heart and spirit the seed of this lie was sown. It was imperative that I repent of having believed this noxious and toxic lie. So I willingly asked for forgiveness and repented of inadvertently agreeing with the enemy most of my life.

Then Mel and Dennis directed me to remain in this picture and to hear the truth. To ask, where Jesus was on the day I was born. This was a new thought to me, that he might have been there. I knew that he was my Saviour but we tend to think that his interested in us only begins when we become Christians. The fuller revelation of this truth was to come to me much later but at that moment I was not holding a theological discussion I was gripped rather by the vivid nature of this picture. It was clarifying more and more as I looked. It became a vision in which I saw my mother laying on a bed about to give birth to me. She was in hospital and there were about four or five people dressed in medical gowns standing around the end of the bed as my mother was about to give birth to me. They had masks and caps on.

As I watched this vision unfold I heard a voice say,

"Now watch this."

I reported what I was seeing to Dennis and he suggested I ask, "Who said that?"

To my amazement and I must say, also my amusement, one of the people in scrubs turned and looked at me, then winked. I did not imagine that winking would happen in a vision.

Then the voice came from behind the mask, "I did!"

I quickly knew what to say and I asked the next question, "Who are you?"

He replied, "I am Jesus! Now watch this" he said again.

I was utterly astonished by this. My attention shifted as the man who had said he was Jesus went through the group and picked up the newly born little boy. The little boy was me!

I heard my mother say, "What is it?"

Jesus held me up in his arms and with a voice full of joy and gladness declared "It's a boy!"

In that moment disappointment vanished out of my life. I knew that I was not a disappointment. While disappointing things happen and I can feel disappointed, I knew because I had seen what Jesus saw that day that I was loved and I was a delight to him.

I asked him, "How do you see me Jesus?"

He answered, "I have waited a long time for this day, you are a joy to me, I rejoiced that day you were born. I knew you before you were born. I knew you were a boy. I created you before you were conceived. You are so precious to me."

As I write this many years after experiencing the vision, I find myself almost reliving this precious vision. I have shared it publicly on many occasions as I have testified to the Father's love for me. Yet as I write I am sensing his favour and love for me right now and I have almost been back in that vision. It seems that today he wants me to see something else that I had not noticed the first time I saw this nearly ten years ago. I hear another voice in the vision. It is the voice of my mother asking, "What is it?" She is told it is a boy and in my spirit I hear her say. "Oh good!"

As I write these words and Linda and I discuss this, sitting as we are beside the River Nile in Uganda, we are reminded of another mother in the Bible who, when her son was born, dedicated him to the Lord. We wondered if that is what my mother had done to me because it was the sort of woman she was. She was most interested in me when I served God. It brought her great joy to know I was serving him. We shall never know the answer to that one. What I do know beyond any shadow of a doubt is that I am not a disappointment. I know God my Father rejoiced over me with singing on the day I was born, that Jesus welcomed me and that the Spirit restored this long forgotten and unseen event to me, so that I would know the truth and by knowing the truth I would be set free. I received a major healing that day and I was open for as much light as I could get into my still wounded heart. Whenever he wanted to shed more light that was fine by me.

~

CHAPTER FIFTEEN

To the Ends of the Earth

~

Dennis and Mel drew us alongside them in their Ministry and we started to accompany them from time to time on weekends and conferences. Along with this they regularly encouraged us to "Go there." By this they meant going to the place where there was still pain in order to let the light of the Holy Spirit shine and bring to the light the cause of the pain in order for there to be healing. We owe them a huge debt of gratitude and are so glad that God brought them into our life at the time he did. Together we spent many days at Church Farm House hearing from the Holy Spirit and allowing Jesus to enter into our dark places and bring light and healing.

Linda had a wonderful healing when, at the end of one session she saw Jesus walking out of the church with his arms around the whole family on that awful night in 1996. On another occasion the Holy

Spirit took me back to the time when I was left as a small child, at Great Ormond Street Children's Hospital in London. I described the events earlier in this book. What I now understood was that I had taken on board a whole load of lies about abandonment and rejection. My interpretation of those events was twisted by the enemy of my soul in order to reinforce the ungodly belief systems that I had developed. Each time I heard Jesus speaking truth to me; that he had always been with me; that he would never and had never abandoned me; that he did not reject me. I heard again that his death on the cross had purified me from all this junk and rubbish and that he had rebuilt me from the inside so that I would see who I really was.

We became members of Big God Ministries board which is the group of people who oversee their ministry and seek to support them. Then eventually they invited us to become full members of their Ministry and they laid hands on us as ministers alongside them.

In 2001 our youngest daughter married an outstanding young man who is a New Zealander, a Kiwi. The wedding was held in a country church in Norfolk and the reception was in a marquee in the garden of Church Farm House. Many came to celebrate with us, including the MDs and John and Susan from Florida. John preached at the wedding ceremony. It was very good that these two couples who have meant so much to us were able to meet for the first time.

Three days after the wedding Mel and Dennis were leading a staff retreat day for the Matthew Project at Church Farm House. During the afternoon session we were interrupted by a phone call from my son, telling me to turn on the TV. I did so and to my horror I saw the first of the Twin Towers of the World Trade Centre collapse in New York. It was 9/11. The MDs were devastated at what was happening to their country as we all watched in disbelief as the terrible events of the day unfolded. Our friends John and Susan were on a plane somewhere over the Atlantic. Their flight was turned back along with thousands of others as America closed its airspace. We spent the week watching the TV and supporting Mel and Dennis who wanted to get home to their families. Three weeks later we were in Florida at John and Susan's. The atmosphere in the US was still very tense everywhere we went. In the middle of this we decided to buy a house in Melbourne, Florida. We planned to use it as a holiday home for the family and rent it out.

Nine months later our youngest daughter and her husband moved to New Zealand and Linda and I promised we would come and visit them there just as soon as we possibly could. We continued to both work full time and also spent weekends ministering with the MDs and managing the extensive gardens at Church Farm House. We wondered, was this what our life was to be now or did God have something else for us?

At the end of 2002 we flew to New Zealand to visit our daughter and her husband. We went for six weeks and had the specific intention of taking time to ask God what he wanted us to do next. My paradigm was that I was a servant and I would obey God and do what he wanted me to do. He was the Master and I was his servant. We both had qualifications that were transportable to just about anywhere in the world. Linda was a highly qualified and experienced nurse and I was a qualified teacher and was theologically trained. I did not know if God would use me in a pastoral role but I was open to it. Lurking in the back of my mind was another ungodly belief that I was on the scrap heap as far as any ministry was concerned. The Morgan-Dohner's ministry revolved around their healing stories and More Light. It was their stories and not ours. We supported them but we did not really have anything to say that was ours. My training at Spurgeon's had taught me to be an exegetical preacher in that I took a passage from the Bible and explained and applied it. We had been taught not to talk about ourselves. So I did not feel I had anything to say. However I was excited by the fact that the More Light approach had a Biblical basis to it rather than a mix of applied psychology and Christian counseling.

We had a wonderful time in New Zealand, we loved the country and the people. Our daughter was clearly very happily settled there. We took time to walk and talk about the 'What next?' question. One day we were at a particularly beautiful beach. I went for a long walk. In one of my More Light sessions with the MDs Jesus had told me he liked to walk and talk with me particularly on the beach! So here I was in the perfect location for a chat about "What next?" It went a bit like this,

"Okay God, here I am, fifty years old. I may have quite a few more years left. I hope so anyway. So what do you want me to do next? Where do you want me to go? I'm available and qualified. You just say the word and I'll do it, because I am your servant and I want to obey you and do what you want. So...?"

Silence. I tried rewording the sentence. I decided I had come over a bit arrogant which I apologised for and tried a more humble approach. Nothing but absolute silence. What was going on? Did he not get the question? After about twenty minutes of this I had a very strange sensation as I felt him say to me,

"Okay Trevor, what would you like to do?"

I was not expecting this and again he called me by my name which was a little unnerving. Initially I thought this was my imagination but the feeling that this was God got stronger and stronger. I also became somewhat irritated.

I blurted out, "What do you mean? 'What do I want to do?' I do what you want to me to do. I am your servant, I've served you or wanted to serve you all my life, haven't I? It's what you want that counts not what I want."

Again a long silence.

Then he said again. "I asked you the question, what do you want to do?"

With a degree of desperation and a slow dawning on me that he was giving me a choice I looked around me at the beautiful beach. I looked at the blue waters of the South Pacific and the golden sands and thought about New Zealand. It was a long way away from the UK. No one knew us there. It meant we weren't viewed with suspicion in certain church circles. It was like going to the Nations or at least the ends of the earth.

So I finally said to God. "I could do this. I could do New Zealand."

Straight away he replied, "Okay leave it with me I'll arrange it!"

I was dumbfounded. God had actually asked me what I would like to do. I thought momentarily, that I should have said Florida or Hawaii.

I told Linda about my conversation. She looked as surprised as I was.

"I see," was all I think she said.

The following week we were staying with the family at a holiday cottage, a bach, in New Zealand parlance. We were touring around and went down the coast one day to a town on the Bay of Plenty. As we drove into the town suddenly the Holy Spirit landed on me in the back of the car. It was most unexpected and I began to shake.

Our daughter, ever the pragmatist, told me to hurry up and listen to what God was saying so we could get on with the day without any more fuss! This certainly got our attention as we drove around the city. We liked the place but nothing much else happened. We went back to Auckland but Linda and I decided we might go to the Bay of Plenty on our own for the weekend just to have a better look around.

We looked on the Partners In Harvest website to see if there was a church there. Partners in Harvest (PIH) was the group of churches and ministries that networked together after the move of God that began in Toronto in 1994. Big God Ministries was a PIH linked ministry. To our surprise there was only one in the whole of New Zealand and it was this town. We looked at each other in amazement. We contacted the church and asked when they met on a Sunday. A rather guarded answer was given which slightly surprised us but we said we were in the area and would see them on Sunday.

We turned up at the church about twenty minutes before things began and were greeted by various people pleased to welcome us. By the time the service had started we had found out that there had been a painful split in recent months. Everyone was very fragile. The leaders were feeling very wounded and exhausted, desperately needing support and encouragement. After the service the couple leading the church invited us to join them for lunch. We spent a couple of hours hearing all their woes and sorrows. They just stopped short of asking us to come and help them. I could almost hear Mel saying, "There's healing for that." Linda and I went and spent the rest of the afternoon on the beach talking about what we had just discovered. We came up with a plan. We would go back and see them the next day and tell them we would be willing to take leave of absence from our jobs and come back to New Zealand on a tourist visa for six months to just be along side them and support them and the church. We prayed about this and had a growing sense that this is what God had in mind too.

We met the next day and they were tremendously excited about all this. They welcomed the idea with great enthusiasm. We agreed to keep in touch. On returning to Auckland we shared the news with our daughter who was a little surprised to say the least. Our plan had evolved and we had decided to sell our house in Florida and buy one in New Zealand that we could use whenever we were over there because at this point we were thinking about coming for six months at a time.

On returning to the UK and sharing this with friends we felt that we should resign from our jobs, go to New Zealand for six months initially and see what God opened up. I went to Florida and sold the house in just a very few days.

All the signs were coming together that suggested we were on track for moving to New Zealand. We had an email from the church telling us how they had received a prophetic word about us coming to them as an assignment from God. All the indicators looked good. I next flew down to New Zealand for two weeks. At the end of this time I had bought a house. It was very quick and very smooth. During my time there the leading couple quizzed me extensively about my Toronto connections and I told them about Big God Ministries. They seemed interested but I got the impression that I had not bought the house in the part of town that they had wanted me to locate to. It was just a passing thought. Dennis and Mel were enthusiastic about our move and felt they were sending us out as team to pioneer the More Light approach to prayer ministry. We planned for them to visit us as soon as they could.

We prepared over the next few months to relocate to New Zealand. We planned on a six month tourist visa which could be extended to nine months. Then we would look at the possibility of getting a work permit based on either of us finding a job. We reduced the contents of Church Farm House to a twenty foot container and shipped it off to New Zealand. We had promised the family in England that we would come back regularly to see them and had a return ticket booked for six months later. Our three parents were all happily settled in old people's homes and we felt a responsibility to regularly return. We also now had a grandchild, our daughter in Newcastle had her first child about the time her sister left for New Zealand.

Contact with the church in New Zealand had become less frequent and when I got a reply to emails they were brief and left us feeling somewhat uncertain of what to expect. The last Sunday in the UK before we flew we were at a Partners in Harvest (PIH) church in Dorset that we had got to know well over the previous few years. We had ministered there several times with the Morgan Dohners. That day they prayed over us and sent us with their blessing. There was lots of prophetic words given to us. Three in particular stood out. The first was that there would be many places where we could place our feet but not all of them were right for us. They felt that lots of opportunities would come our way but that we would carefully need to only step into those that God had prepared. The second was to do with the orphan spirit or attitude of heart. We had not come across this terminology before. Essentially we were told we would experience this spirit but God would also reveal the truth to us too. Finally the third was based around the number of volcanos in New Zealand. The woman who had this picture said she felt the first place that we went to would be an extinct volcano. The second place we went to would be an active volcano. She felt God saying that the first place we went to our ministry would be dormant or extinct but the second place it would be active and erupt. This was a vivid picture which we have often thought about in the years since we moved to New Zealand.

We arrived and spent the first few days in Auckland with the family and then went to the house we had bought. This was going to be the first time that Linda had seen the house! We contacted the church leaders and asked if they knew somewhere we could stay the first night as we only had air mattresses. It would be like camping! They suggested a motel. That was unexpected because I had stayed with them in their home before. Anyway we arrived and began sorting things out. We went to the church on the first Sunday and were greeted warmly by a number of people we had met at Christmas time. The leaders just said, "So you are here then!"

Within a very few days it became painfully apparent that they had changed their minds about us. The church had grown even smaller and had since pulled out of PIH. The leaders were extremely defensive and suspicious of us. They told us they had just finished a three month teaching series on the Jezebel spirit. This surprised me as I wondered why so much time should be given to such an obscure topic. They then said that a new series would begin on the following Sunday on Biblical Leadership. So we went to the church that week with interest about what would be shared. There was a sense of the presence of God in the church during the worship which was being led by a very open and sensitive woman. Many were being touched where they sat. Then the leader got up to say that the Holy Spirit was moving at the front and if we wanted to receive more then we had to go to the front. If we stayed in our seats the Spirit would not bless us. Alarm bells were ringing in our heads.

Then the other leader's wife began to teach the biblical leadership series.

The first sign of a biblical leader was that they would recognise an Absalom spirit, the spirit of a usurper who would come into the church. She described Absalom, David's son as a tall, good looking, fair haired man. The couple sitting next to us who we had got to know laughed and said to me, "Sounds like she is describing you!" This was meant to be a joke and then he looked at me and said. "OMG she is!!!" There then followed twelve indicators to identify such a spirit and a thirteenth one for good measure that said an Absalom spirit would refuse to acknowledge any one of the aforementioned twelve.

We went home for lunch hardly able to believe what we had just heard. I sent an email to Dennis and Mel describing the morning. I had a very quick one sentence reply from Dennis. "RUN, RUN FOR YOUR LIVES." We did. We stopped attending the church much to the relief of the leaders. We kept in touch with a couple who we had met at the church who hung on for a few months before they left. Sadly the church closed a few months later.

The following months were very pleasant and enjoyable. We took the opportunity that this gave us to travel around and met a variety of people. We made friends with a couple, Murray and Julie, who ran a small Baptist Church, whose son was on staff at Toronto Airport Christian Fellowship. They were linked with PIH in an informal way. A trip back to the UK coincided with my father's death so I was able to help my mother and brother with the funeral. In New Zealand sometime later we moved house to a lifestyle block just outside of Tauranga, were we had pigs and chickens and worked with a small local charity. This enabled us to get a work permit.

Linda secured a job working at a Hospice and this enabled us to get residency. So at the end of nine months we were more or less settled in New Zealand.

Melanie and Dennis came in the first year for a visit and we introduced them to Murray and Julie. They were there when we held a house warming party at our new house. Through another contact at the party they ended up getting an invitation to speak at a church that had been flowing in the Toronto renewal for a number of years. The following year the MDs returned. By then we had started attending this church called the Red Shed and had got to know the leaders well. We had been invited to join them on the leadership team and we were settling into life in New Zealand. On visits back to the UK we met two new grandchildren and also welcomed our first one in New Zealand. Sadly both my parents died during the first couple of years and Linda's mother developed Alzheimer's disease. On trips back to the UK we continued to minister with Mel and Dennis joining them on a trip to the Ukraine on one occasion.

~

CHAPTER SIXTEEN

And Back Again!

~

We went into business in New Zealand with the leader of our church. It was a publishing company that produced lifestyle magazines. It was a great idea and I thoroughly enjoyed the opportunity it gave me to write. I wrote a monthly column about seeing life in New Zealand through a Pom's eyes. Pom is the name given to ex pat Brits in New Zealand. We also started building our own house near the beach in Papamoa. We had gradually sold off the houses in the UK and brought all our assets to New Zealand. Then we heard that Sanna and her husband, who was a pastor, were moving to New Zealand to lead a church plant into Auckland. Our centre of family focus had definitely shifted to the antipodes. Our son was even considering applying to join the police in NZ too. In many ways life was very good.

Through the Morgan Dohners we heard that a Kiwi couple called James and Denise Jordan who lead Fatherheart Ministries had recently returned to New Zealand and had set up their base in Taupo. They too were a Partners In Harvest ministry. We shared this with the couple we were in business with and planned a visit to Taupo to meet the Jordans at their base, called the Eden Centre.

We four were staying in Taupo over the Christmas holiday and contacted James and Denise Jordan. We were invited to lunch to meet them and their team. The Eden Centre was a three bedroom bungalow set in five acres of beautifully laid out gardens just outside Taupo. The previous occupiers of the property had been owners of a garden centre and florist shop. As a result they had constructed a very beautiful exotic English style garden in Taupo. It looked and felt very familiar to our eyes. James and Denise welcomed us warmly. I remember looking at James and seeing his eyes. There was something about the way he looked at me that made me feel both slightly uncomfortable and drawn in at the same time. It was very disarming.

He wanted to show us around the garden. I really loved the garden. I asked who did the gardening and James said they didn't have a gardener but needed one. A random thought crossed my mind. It was that I would love to be the gardener at the Eden Centre but Taupo was two hours from Papamoa and out of the question. They shared with us their story of how they had set up Fatherheart Ministries. They told how they had travelled for many years with Jack Winter, teaching the biblical truth that God is our real father and we are his sons and daughters. They told how the Father had provided the money supernaturally to buy the Eden Centre and hence their move back to New Zealand. Their continual use of the term Father or THE Father, rather than God, I found unusual. It sounded so intimate and familiar yet at the same time very odd to my ears. I knew God is God the Father but it was not what I called him. The most intimate I ever came up with was Lord.

We met their team too and we promised to keep in touch. A weekend visit from their team was planned for later in the year in Papamoa at the Red Shed. In the mean time we had a visit planned to go back to the UK which was business related as we had published a magazine for incoming British migrants to New Zealand. We were at an exhibition in London promoting New Zealand and were also distributing this magazine. This aspect of business life meant we regularly returned to Britain and were able to keep in touch with the remaining family there.

This visit back to the UK coincided with the one hundred and fiftieth anniversary of the founding of Spurgeon's College. There was a great celebration planned at the college and all former students were invited. I had not been back to Spurgeon's for thirty years since my graduation in 1976. It also coincided therefore with the thirtieth anniversary of the ordination to Christian ministry of the group of men I had trained with. It was decided to hold a reunion together in the afternoon of the main events. Linda and I felt that this was a good opportunity to attend.

However I did not expect to meet God that day at Spurgeon's. It was with some degree of trepidation that we went back to my old college. It had been ten years since the disclosure that led to my resignation. Ten years before I had declined the invitation to attend the twentieth reunion because I was broken, embarrassed and ashamed. Now ten years later I was still hurting somewhat on the inside and wondering if I would ever be in ministry again. Something inside was saying I was on God's scrapheap. That I had blown it and there were no second chances. Maybe the lack of openings in ministry was God's way of punishing me. While these thoughts do not agree with the biblical concept of grace or forgiveness, in my heart

I wondered if indeed I was no longer on God's active list. That I was no longer needed. I didn't want to meet too many people who would ask things like, "Where are you ministering now?" Nonetheless we decided to go to the College celebrations and reunion and just see how we would get on.

I took a deep breath as we walked through the main doors of the College and headed into the crowds of people. There were many familiar faces. The first couple who turned and walked towards us were from the church I had grown up in. This was Peter whose father had taken me out preaching when I was a teenager. He was about ten years older than I.

His wife greeted us by saying, "It's Trevor, the naughty boy!"

Suddenly I was back in my childhood days. "I've had healing for that." I replied.

Mel and Dennis had sorted that one out quite well some time ago. However it took me back to the beginning of my Christian journey.

Within moments we met another significant person. Bryan Gilbert had been the pastor of Linda's home church and had introduced her to Jesus and baptised her. He had been the chaplain at the Boy's Brigade camp where I had my fifth and final conversion experience when I was thirteen years old. He had been involved in our wedding and was also one of those who had laid hands on me when I was ordained as a Baptist Minister thirty years before. This took me back to my call from God into ministry. He was so delighted to see us and he asked if we would sit with him for the banquet later that day. We willingly agreed. Towards the end of the meal he asked if he could pray for us. He took both our hands in his and prayed there at the table. In his prayer it was as if he was reconfirming our calling. He prayed back into me things that had been taken from me, that I had lost and that had been stolen. It was as if God was reaffirming me and telling me I was not on the scrap heap. That he had not withdrawn either the call on my life or his blessing on that call. I was very tearful.

During the afternoon we had our reunion of the men who had all graduated the same year from College. It was thirty years. Not all were there. A couple had died and a few had lost contact. There were about twelve of us and I had not seen some of them since we left College. A few knew of the troubles we had experienced ten years earlier. I had declined to join the twentieth anniversary reunion because it was all too raw. Now I felt I had enough courage to be with them. We took a group photo which eventually was circulated among us under the caption, 'Change and decay all around I see!' It said it all really.

When we had settled down, one of the guys who was now the vice principal at the College, suggested we share together what had been the defining moment of our thirty years in ministry. I sat there and my first thought was that there was no way I was going to share what mine was.

One by one as we listened to each other speak. The common thread that united us, without exception, was that the defining moment for each of us had been one of pain. A child that died, a grown daughter that was killed in an accident, the rejection of a church after several hard years of ministry, the death of a spouse, the pain of betrayal. So it went on until it came to my turn. I told them what had happened to me. The fall from grace, the moral failure and the pain that it had brought to us both. The rejection that I felt and the abandonment by friends and former colleagues. We all shared a common experience. Pain, deep wounding pain, and here we all were sitting looking at each other with understanding and compassion. Chris, the leader led in prayer and he used the expression, 'We are but servants'. I thought about it and it summed up what I was, who I thought I was. I am a servant who must obey orders from the Master. I just needed to make sure I knew what his orders were and if he still wanted me. We prayed for each other and we shook hands, very English. It was a cathartic and healing moment for me.

That evening there was the celebration thanksgiving service. There were many people attending whom I recognised. At the end of the service I stood chatting with two of the men from my year and suddenly I saw someone approaching who I had not seen for many years. My stomach twisted and the blood drained from my face. One of the guys asked me if everything was alright as it looked as if I had seen a ghost. "Indeed I have but it is no ghost." The man who had been party to my fall fifteen years before stood in front of us and greeted us. Instantly the two men put two and two together and came up with right number. Brief words were exchanged and he walked away. I was literally trembling. In my heart I felt a great sadness and compassion for him. I felt no animosity. I wanted to just bless him. The two men stood on either side of me and put their hands on my shoulders and one said, "You are always welcome here. You are our brother."

Most of the day I had been fighting back tears. We needed to leave and we returned to our friend's home where we were staying in South London. I really needed time to process what had happened that day. It seemed that God had taken me deliberately and purposefully right back to the beginning of my Christian life, to my conversion, my call to ministry, my ordination and my fall from grace. He also seemed to want to reaffirm me each step of the way, to restore my sense of calling, and remind me that the call still stood and that he had a future for me as a servant. He even tested my heart to see if there was unforgiveness there. I was surrounded all day by affirming words of his loving grace for me. I saw that I had not only fallen from grace but I had fallen into his grace which was far bigger, richer and more wonderful than I had ever imagined or known.

As part of the trip back in Europe we spent a few days in Switzerland staying with a Vineyard Pastor who had been an Intern at our church in Norfolk some years earlier. On this visit we joined him and his entire leadership team at a party given to thank them for their service through the previous twelve months. I was asked to share something at the end of the evening. Throughout the evening one after another talked about serving God with all their might. I decided to speak from John 15 verse 15 where Jesus says,

> *"I no longer call you servants, because a servant does not know his master's business. Instead I have called you friends, for everything I have learned from my Father I have made known to you."*

My point was that we can so easily get caught up with doing the work of God and miss the relationship with him. It was a jolly good talk and straight out of my head. It wasn't in my heart since I was the classic servant myself. I was in mid flow when I had one of those moments which others who have ever preached may recognise. I found myself being interrupted by God.

I felt him say in my spirit. "That's interesting, Trevor, but are you my friend?"

I was somewhat taken aback by the question and felt myself

responding inside by saying, "Of course I'm your friend, I wouldn't be doing this for you otherwise. Can't we talk about this later I am trying to preach here."

This exchange happened in a split second but I knew that God had caught me out red handed! I did not have a clue if I was a friend or not. To be a friend implies that you like someone. This meant that he was talking about whether we liked each other. I loved him because that what good Christians do, but like him? More to the point did he like me? There were still major parts of me that I didn't like so I couldn't imagine that he really liked me. I assumed as he was God, he probably did like me, but that was his job, to like us wretched sinners, well at least to love us. This experience left me feeling rather uneasy.

On returning to the UK from Switzerland I had lots to think about. As we always did, we visited Linda's mum who was in the early stages of Alzheimer's Disease and spent time with our son. My mother had died the previous year. We also always spent a couple of days with friends during which we would pray together about what God was doing in each other's lives. They had visited us in New Zealand and had been very supportive over the years. We had been in New Zealand for four years. I was feeling that whilst it was all very comfortable and enjoyable we were just not in any way doing anything for God. These friends at one point had asked us to go back to the UK to work with them in their church. I was tempted but really did not know what to do. In the light of all the reaffirmation I had received from God at Spurgeon's and his unsettling question to me in Switzerland.

There was a lot on my list to talk to him about.

When it came to my turn for prayer with the four of us, at the top of my mind was the thought, did God want me to go back to New Zealand to serve him in some way there? If he did, we needed to have a better understanding how and in what context because it was not working out at this point. Being in the business was fine but it was making a big hole in my pocket and that needed to be sorted out too. Had I got it wrong? What did he want? So when we got to praying, as was our custom, we tended to ask the Holy Spirit to lead us as we asked him questions.

I went straight to the issue in hand and asked. "Okay God, do you want me to go back to New Zealand to serve you?"

Immediately I felt God answer me in my spirit. I know it was God because I would never have thought up this answer.

He said, "I don't want you to go back to New Zealand as a servant because I have enough servants in New Zealand already."

I was shocked by this. How could that be? Servant was what I did, it is who I was. I had done servant all my Christian life, what is more I did servant extremely well. It was my default setting. If in doubt, I serve. This was alarming to say the least. I quickly followed this up with another clarifying question. This is something else we had learned from the MDs. If you don't understand something God says, ask another question to clarify what you are hearing.

"So what do you want me to do?" I asked.

Again, almost immediately, I heard in my spirit his reply "I want you to go back to New Zealand as a son, because I don't have many sons in New Zealand."

This was truly shocking to me. The shocking part was two fold. First the clarity with which I heard his voice and secondly the realisation that I had no idea what it meant. So again I responded almost angrily, "But I don't know how to do son!" This was the whole issue about why I was angry. I had no idea of what it looked like to be a son to God. It implied I would need to relate to him as a son and him as my Father. I had not done that. I had shut down to my dad many years before and had not related to him with the heart of a son. I just did not know how to relate to God as a son. I assumed it was something else I had to do now.

Then I heard his voice again. He did not react to my anger but he answered so gently and with such a kind tone. "If you let me I will show you how to be a son."

I did not notice at the time that he talked about being a son. My hasty conclusion was that son was something else I had to do and I did not know how to do it.

We returned to New Zealand and I was not happy. All this talk of son was new to me. It seemed like I was being given a whole new set of hoops to jump through to be acceptable to God. It was a busy time. We were in the final stages of finishing our lovely beach house with the swimming pool in Papamoa. The business was quite stressful and as an investor along with others we were always being asked for more injections of cash. The cash was getting quite low too and this was adding to the stress. Church life was not satisfying and I had resigned as a leader some months before as I did not have any confidence in the leader who was also the managing director of the business.

The Church had a Fatherheart weekend coming up being led by a team from Fatherheart Ministries in Taupo. The Jordans had sent five of their team for the weekend. To be frank, I wondered what they would say all weekend as there were about six sessions planned. Also it occurred to me , somewhat arrogantly that there really couldn't be that much to say about the fatherhood of God that I couldn't read in a good theological book and probably also a lot more coherently. Then again it would be good to see them because there was something very attractive about these people that I couldn't put my finger on.

The weekend was surprisingly good. They kept on talking about the heart. This was a little bit annoying as I was looking for some meaty stuff to make me think rather than this continual reference to our hearts. Then there were the looks. I kept noticing them looking at people in a slightly, how shall I put it, dopey way! I could see where this was all going. There was going to come the moment when someone would come up to me, give me the look and then tell me that the Father really loved me.

I really didn't want to hear that. If God couldn't somehow tell me himself that he loved me I did not want to hear it second hand from anybody else. Suddenly, like a sulky, orphan hearted little boy, I was back at home hearing people tell me how much my dad loved me. Back then I needed to hear him to say he loved me, I did not want to hear it from someone else, second hand. He just was never able to say those words to me. Dad may have felt it, but he could not express it. He lived in a generation who found such things embarrassing and difficult. I can't remember either of my parents ever saying it in my hearing to each other and certainly never to me as a child. I needed to hear it and because I never did, I assumed that he didn't really love me.

Then it happened. The ministry time began and the team were beginning to cruise the room with that look in their eyes. One of the guys was heading towards me with an earnest look that I was sure would include 'the Father loves you' statement. As he approached I just couldn't help myself. I knew if he said this to me I might even punch him. So I put my hand up in his face in front of me.

I said, "Jan, don't you dare tell me that the Father loves me, because I just don't believe it. If he can't tell me himself I just don't want to know. I'm sick and tired of hearing all this stuff second hand. I need him to tell me himself."

Jan looked slightly shocked but in a way that said he was not surprised by my reaction. Jesus said once, "Out of the mouth the heart speaks." I had done exactly that and the truth was out there. Jan replied, "I wasn't going to say that to be honest. All I was thinking of saying was that we have a week long School coming up in about three months time and I wondered if you and Linda would like to come."

I was standing there wishing I could reel those words back in like a fishing line, but I had said them and the state of my heart was exposed. Jan put his arm around my shoulder and said, "You might just hear him tell you that he loves you too. You never know. Give it some thought."

What could I say? It was as if I had thrown the gauntlet down at God's feet. If he was a Father, if he was a Father to me, he needed to tell me, I needed him to tell me. I was not going to settle for anything second hand or fake. If this was part of the process of 'doing son' then it is what I wanted and what I needed. I was too tired to argue and start all over again. I was worn out trying to please him, beating myself up all the time when I failed. If he was Father then I needed to know what that meant and I had a few things to discuss with him about the way fathers behaved towards their children.

∼

CHAPTER SEVENTEEN

Meeting My Real Father

~

Three months later we were driving to the northern New Zealand town of Kaitaia for a Fatherheart Ministries 'A' School led by James and Denise Jordan and some of their team from Taupo. It was called an 'A' School because the second school was called a 'B' School. That is typical Kiwi logic and simplicity. In the weeks leading up to the School I had vacillated about wanting to go. I had a longing to know God as Father but at the same time I was afraid of opening up old wounds. I had moved to the place of knowing that I did not know God as my Father, not in a real way. I knew this theologically but at another level I was still afraid of God, like Adam, because I felt ashamed and was wearing my fig leaves. This was not the language that I was using at the time but it describes what was going on in my heart.

The first session started on Sunday evening and James suggested that we did not need to take notes as only the things that God has written on our hearts would stay with us. The notes we write usually stay on the shelf. I rebelliously decided I would take notes!

James is a speaker who teaches prophetically from his heart. He is engagingly easy to listen to and you feel like you are drinking in the message he is speaking. At the same time he is shockingly provocative, like a blacksmith hammering out the steel, blow after blow, until the metal is forged in the fire. A week of this was going to be exhausting!

As he began to teach that first night he said that God wanted to change our hearts. As he did that then we would become different people.

Did I want to become a different person? Before I had time to digest this thought, James was saying God doesn't have to try to love us, he was loving us already with his whole heart. He was changing us to be like him. Church had traditionally demanded that we do, we act, we behave in a certain way in order to be good Christians. James said that God wanted us to be like him without working or acting like it. God didn't want us to act. He did not want us to even get our act together because if we did it would still only be an act. Ouch! That hit the spot. God wanted to change out hearts so that we automatically become like Jesus without any effort or striving. So that we are like him without thinking about it. This was shockingly relevant because that is exactly what I had been doing most of my Christian life. This was with the best intentions, but I was exhausted by it. In the notes, which I was not supposed to be writing, I wrote, "I ask you to change my heart...Father." This was the first tentative time I wrote that description of him and addressing him as Father. It felt somewhat contrived and did not come naturally to me. Nonetheless

I wrote it, looked at it and thought I would see what happened.

I began to see that the revelation of the fatherheart of God was a key part in the move of the Spirit that had began in Toronto although I had missed it at the time. The leaders at the Toronto church had talked about the Father's Blessing but nearly all of my experiences at Toronto over the years following were more to do with manifestations of the Spirit. Speakers I had heard over the years from Toronto had said that this was evidence that the Father loved us. I began to see that whilst some aspects of this were true the revelation of the Father's love went very much deeper. I knew about it at a head level but the revelation went way deeper than my knowledge and experience at that time. I was beginning to hunger and long for the Father to take me much deeper than my current understanding of his love.

During the week it was said that if our human father's love was not available to us or the things he did were not appropriate, then we so often close ourselves from that source of love. This can result in closing our hearts off to the love of God as a Father to us as well. We begin to feel we don't need it because we have managed at some level without it. It dawned on me that I had closed my heart to my dad's love. As a result I had also closed my heart to God the Father's love for me.

My heart was very vulnerable. I had been lied to by the devil. My heart was easily hurt and I had closed it to protect it from more pain and hurt. By closing my heart down to protect myself I made it very difficult to open it up to God's love for me. I had not been able to receive love from my father or mother partly because they had difficulty expressing it and partly because I closed myself off to it. Yet I still needed that love. The result was a love deficit in my emotions. My heart was open to Jesus and particularly to the Holy Spirit but I could not open my heart to God as Father.

I wrote in my notes, "Father, reveal your heart to me this week. Unblock the blockages in my understanding that have stopped me receiving your love, not for the sake of ministry or anointing but for the sheer joy of knowing you."

The teaching over the next few days was reassuringly biblical and rooted in classic Christian theological truth but it was presented entirely differently. Whilst my mind was stimulated and enriched, my heart became engaged in a very different way. In one session a verse from John 14 was mentioned that I had never noticed before. I had studied John's Gospel while I was at Spurgeon's. I had translated it from Greek and studied it in detail but I do not recall ever really noticing this verse. It was John 14 verse 18 where Jesus says to his disciples,

"I will not leave you as orphans I will come to you."

It is not known if the disciples were physically orphans or not, certainly James and John were not since their parents are mentioned in the Gospels. So it seems that Jesus was meaning that in some way the disciples and all of us behaved like orphans or in an orphan-hearted way.

This orphan-like behaviour was described as an orphan spirit, not a spirit that needs to be cast out but an attitude of heart. I suddenly remembered the prophetic word given to us when we first left the UK some years before that we would experience this spirit, but that God would also reveal the truth to us. The only way we could remove this orphan spirit was to replace it with the love of the Father and receive the spirit of sonship. This was new to me. I had never considered these two different spirits or rather attitudes of heart.

I began to see looking back over my years as a Christian and a church leader that many of the problems we had experienced were rooted in this orphan-like attitude. Being born again had not taken it away, only the love of the Father could do that. I began to see that much of contemporary Christian thinking, behaviour and leadership style in our churches comes from a place of orphan-heartedness. For example we can so often act like orphans because of the pain in our hearts. Consequently we may treat our brothers and sisters very badly. At one point the gospel was described as being about an orphan spirit that was overcome by a spirit of being sons. Jesus came to bring us out of orphan-heartedness to becoming brothers and to be like him as sons of God the Father. This was a new thought that was sinking into my heart.

I was beginning to see that in my own case I had acted in a orphan-like way on many occasions. This was true in the way my identity was tied to what I did rather than who I am. When my identity was taken away from me at the time I was removed from ministry in 1996 I did not know who I was. I had always driven myself in order to validate who I was by any ministry I had or performed. I liked the reputation I had as a successful pastor and leader but when I lost it, I was deeply wounded and lost because I did not know how to function as a son. I had never much bothered about titles but I could see how the Christian world is full of ridiculous titles, all designed to validate ourselves. Jesus was a son who heard his Father's voice and only spoke his Father's words. He did not need to be called by any particular title. I was surprised again because I had never noticed how often Jesus said he only said the things he heard his Father

201

saying and did the things he saw his Father doing.

I was seeing very clearly how orphan spirited Christianity thinks of God as the commander, the unknowable order giver, the great authority on everything. It is focused on submission and obedience. I could hear myself asking God to just tell me what to do and I would do it. No wonder he was silent that time on the beach in New Zealand. I was like an orphan waiting for orders not a son asking Father where he is working. Obedience is only an issue when we don't really want to do as we are told. I had wanted to obey God but this was driven by fear and a desire to seek his approval. Orphan heartedness is focused on servanthood which explains why the Father told me he did not want me to return to New Zealand as a servant but as a son. Sons, I was discovering, want to please their Father and cooperate with what he is doing. It is doing what he loves to do and in harmony with him rather than doing what they are told to do. Seeing myself as a servant and often serving out of compulsion was so much how I had lived. I wanted to hear him say to me, "Well done good and faithful servant". I wanted his approval, to receive his blessing, his recognition and the recognition of others. My hunger for ministry and the desire to build a ministry was yet another expression of this orphan heartedness that I had lived in for so long.

It was becoming clear to me that sons are able to serve their Father and rest in his love and see this not as a duty but a joy and a privilege. The Father wants us to serve him simply because we love him. He would not love us any less if we never served him again or did anything for him. This was such a shocking thought because so much of our Christianity is works and faith based, but not love based.

I heard a quote some time ago attributed to Bill Johnson from Redding California who was reported to have said: "The Father loves us as much when we are raising the dead as when we are taking a nap!". The reality is that sons delight to work alongside their Father and participate with him in his works. Sons look forward to hearing, "Welcome home son." In ministry sons esteem brothers and sisters and want to help them into ministry and be a blessing rather than get blessed themselves. The ministry gifts described in Ephesians 4 of apostle, prophet, pastor, teacher and evangelist can be operated out of an orphan heart. When this is the case they have caused great difficulty and sadness in the church often wounding many and contributing to hundreds of thousands of people abandoning church life. I reflected on my years in two streams of church life that described themselves as apostolic and began to see that many of the problems that emerged in those movements were orphan-like in origin. Whilst they had grasped wonderful aspects of truth they had sometimes been administered it in an orphan-like way.

On the other hand, evangelist sons know how to reveal the Father to the lost. Teachers who know they are sons teach life through the Father because they hear what Father is saying. Pastors who are sons minister life because they are full of compassion and comfort. They have experienced this for themselves from the Father of compassion and the God of all comfort as the Paul describes him in 2 Corinthians Chapter 1 verse 4. They know how to receive comfort themselves from the Father and are able to give his comfort to others.

Prophets who know they are sons speak as Jesus spoke, only saying what they hear their Father saying. They do not need to play the part of a prophet or act as a bizarre caricature of an Old Testament prophet.

Apostles are first and foremost sons who are doing the works that they see the Father doing, going where they see him going, and laying a foundation in all things that is based on the revelation of God as their Father. They cooperate with their older brother Jesus as he builds his church rather than being driven to build a church of their own orphan-like making. Apostles who have the heart of a son are not interested in their own kingdoms but only their Father's kingdom.

I reflected on the question, "Who are you?" which we encouraged people to ask when ministering the More Light model. We needed to ask this question because so many did not know and could not distinguish God's voice, from the devil's voice or their own voice. When we come to know the Father's voice, through intimate relationship, we don't need to ask that question anymore. Many people are still on that journey and it is important that they learn to hear his voice. The whole ministry approach of More Light was taking on new significance as I began to see how orphan-heartedness was at the root of so many of our issues. It was like a large missing piece of my jigsaw was being put into place.

Up to 1997 James Jordan had been saying that this was one of the many messages that needed to be taught. Many had begun teaching the revelation of the Father's love. Then in Holland he came to see that this was not just another book on the shelf but was the shelf itself. The shelf on which every other truth in the Bible stood.

Everything began to be seen as a manifestation of the Father's love. The cross itself which is considered the central point of all truth was in fact an expression of the Father's love, if not the greatest expression. It was because of the Father's love for the world, that he sent his Son. Grace, which is prized by so many, is no grace at all if it is not founded on the love of the Father. Grace that is not ministered out of the loving heart of the Father is just another version of law dressed up as grace, but with no heart. Sons operate out of a place of being loved whereas the orphan-hearted may talk about grace but in reality love the law and strict adherence to the law. This was not just a message of the Father's love for us. It was a revelation.

Teaching that has no manifestation of the Father's heart is not going to be revelation. This manifestation is real and is recognisable experientially. It is not sentimentality that has no back bone, it is solid and recognisable. It was said at one point that if we did not have a revelation of Father's love, all our other teaching and ministry would be slightly warped. It is not that God would not use it, it would just not be the whole truth.

James quoted Derek Prince, one of the twentieth centuries most important Christian teachers, who in 1998 wrote about an experience of the Father's love he had two years earlier.

Prince wrote, "My understanding of God as father was revolutionized by a personal experience early in 1996. My wife Ruth and I had been sitting in bed one morning, praying together as we normally do. Suddenly I became aware of a powerful force at work in me... my whole body was forcefully shaken by it. Immediately, without any mental process of reasoning, I knew that I could call God my Father. I had used the phrase "our Father" for more than fifty years. Doctrinally, I was clear about this truth. I had even preached a series of three messages on "Knowing God as Father". What I received at that moment was a direct, personal revelation. From that morning, it became natural for me to address God as 'Father' or 'my Father'. I had a personal relationship, not just a theological position." (Derek Prince Teaching Newsletter Mar/Apr 1998)

As the week unfolded I became aware that the reason I did not know the reality of this revelation was not because the Father did not love me, but rather something was in the way. James kept saying that the Father was loving us right at that moment. Where there was a struggle it was because there was something standing in the way blocking us from receiving his love. There were things that were hindering the revelation from coming to us. I began to reflect on what had been stopping me.

Ever since I had received the word from God about going back to New Zealand as a son everything had stopped. It was as if I had nothing to say until I received the revelation of the Father's love for me personally. Without this in my life it would only be a repetition of past truth, of stale bread. God had used me in the past but now he had so much more for me. I began to see that God as Father wanted to make it real for us. I began to see that God was already a Father to ME and he desperately wanted to make this real in my heart. He was already loving me but the blockages stopped me from experiencing it.

≈

CHAPTER EIGHTEEN

An Axe
at the Root

~

In the middle of the week James shared about his own relationship with his dad. He had a father who was similar to my own but James' reaction had been different from mine. However, to be able to deal with my reaction to my dad it would involve forgiveness. I had been there so many times with forgiving my father. How many times did I have to forgive him? I did not want to dishonour his memory but I had to be honest with myself and how I felt.

Time after time I found myself trying to forgive him for the same things. There was still pain in many memories. Added to that there was guilt associated that said I shouldn't feel like this. To even think like this I felt was unloving and not honouring of him. I was a Christian who was supposed to be mature and not behaving like that. Even though he had died a few years before in some ways I still felt I had him by the throat and was holding him responsible for much of my stuff.

Then came the real hammer blow on the anvil of my heart. I had to forgive him again, not just by choosing to do so as an act of the will but from my heart. In the past we had been taught that if we do not forgive then we will not be forgiven. This clearly is not biblical but it is a widely held view and believed by many. It is rooted in a lie of the devil which makes our salvation and forgiveness dependent on what we have to do rather than in what Jesus accomplished on the cross. It is a gospel of works rather than grace.

Forgiveness was the issue that Peter raised with Jesus in Matthew chapter 18 verse 21.

"How many times must I forgive my brother when he sins against me? Up to seven times?"

I sympathised with his feelings. Jesus' answer of seventy-seven times was saying it is beyond human capacity. Forgiveness itself is a grace gift and comes from the heart not an act of the will. The whole parable that he told shows that forgiveness is an issue of the heart. Gritted teeth forgiveness from the will is just a veneer. Forgiveness from the heart runs much deeper. I was galvanised by this. I knew that this was one of the roots of my issues. I was on the edge of my seat. I had heard countless talks and sermons about forgiveness and I had preached my fair share of them but this was different. Here was a man who was speaking from his heart, from the heart of the Father right into my heart. In the parable in Matthew 18 Jesus says the kingdom of heaven is like a king who wants to settle his accounts. The kingdom of heaven or the kingdom of God is that place where the Father's love is being poured out and manifested. Unlike some parables where each part is allegorical, this parable is about the principle of forgiving from the heart as Jesus says in verse 35. So the king in the story does not represent God as can be seen by the way he deals with his servants. If we confuse the king with God we end up with a gospel of works rather than grace.

The king represents us. The king decided to settle his accounts with his servants. He wanted to find out who owed him anything and then he called in the debts. He found one man who owed him millions. This was a huge theft. When someone sins against us they are in reality stealing something from us. Therefore they owe us. When someone does not give us what we are owed or they have not done what they are supposed to do, they are stealing from us or robbing us. It is not saying it does not matter what has happened to us. Rather the opposite, we are taking an account of exactly what has been owed to us or what has been stolen. It immediately raised the question, what had been stolen from me? If we do not know what has been stolen from us then we cannot forgive. Unforgiveness is the same as demanding repayment, whereas forgiveness is canceling the debt, paying the price to let them off the debt. In order to forgive from the heart I needed to understand what had been stolen from me. In addition, forgiveness is not complete until our hearts have released all the issues.

I found myself thinking about the issue of forgiveness towards my parents particularly my father. They were not able to give me what I needed, they could not give of themselves emotionally in the way I needed. They had done the best they could and I am grateful for that. However, even if they had been the best parents in the world there would still be love deficits as no one is perfect.

Discovering this was a key part of the process of forgiving and living in the Father's love. The servant in the story could not pay the debt, (verse 25). Even if he and his whole family were sold there would not be enough to pay the debt that was owed. Those who have sinned against us can never pay us back, they do not have the ability to pay us back. My parents were unable to pay me back! My parents were unable to be what I needed them to be. They too had not received the love they needed either.

The enemy of our souls, the devil, has attacked us constantly to rob, destroy and kill. He is a liar and is robbing us of every kind and loving action and thought in order to destroy and kill everything of our humanity. This has happened to us all, including our parents. We are all emotionally wounded to some degree.

When the servant started to beg for mercy he was trying to think of everything he could do to pay back the debt, but he just could not do it. The king, seeing this, took pity on him. The word translated as pity is also the word for compassion. When we begin to have compassion on the one who owes us, we can begin to forgive. A dictionary definition of compassion describes a feeling of deep sympathy and sorrow for another who is stricken by misfortune accompanied by a strong desire to alleviate the suffering. The definition of pity says it is sympathetic or kindly sorrow evoked by the suffering, distress, or misfortune of another, often leading to giving relief, aid or to show mercy. Both are heart felt responses and are characteristics of the Father. He is the Father of compassion. If we love mercy rather than judgement we won't have a problem in forgiving as we see what the devil has done in our own parent's lives. When compassion comes it shows we are more concerned about the one who has sinned against us than the offence we carry in our hearts. This sets us free to forgive them and love them as we set them free.

In the second half of the parable Jesus describes an encounter between this newly forgiven servant and another. In the same way that the king represented us in the first part of the story in the second part the servant represents us. The main point of the first part has been what forgiveness from the heart looks like. The main point is what happens to us if we do not forgive from our hearts. When the servant who had his debt cancelled by the king met another servant who owed him a much smaller amount, he did not have compassion but instead he grabbed him by the throat. (v 28). He demanded payment and would not forgive the man. If we do not let go of those who have sinned against us we are in reality waiting for a repayment that probably will not come. We can hold on to it and become bitter and resentful towards them. It is as if we want to punish them, to make them drink the bitter cup of poison that they deserve but instead we drink it ourselves. Some times the unforgiveness defines us and we are afraid to let it go lest we lose our identity. When our hearts are still connected in unforgiveness to our earthly fathers and mothers then our hearts are blocked in receiving the love of the Father.

When Jesus describes the king as giving the unforgiving servant over to the torturers this describes what we are like in our hearts, tortured by the loss and pain and destroyed by bitterness. This does not mean that God the Father punishes us, tortures us and refuses to forgive us. Instead, because we have chosen to live in that place of unforgiveness and self torture, he is unable to help us until we repent.

Many Christians who know their sins are forgiven, struggle to forgive others. They are born again but are so often stuck in their Christian walk. If our salvation was dependent on forgiving others we move back into a works based gospel. It would nullify the availability of the forgiveness that Jesus bought for us on the cross.

One of the most immediate consequences was that I had compassion welling up inside me for my parents and the brokenness they must have experienced in their lives. Forgiveness began to be much easier. In my mind's eye I would reach out my hand as if to touch them and bless them and declare that they owe me nothing and picture myself extending forgiveness to them. At times I would weep when I saw how they had suffered. Every time I have heard this teaching, it is as if the Father peels back another layer to take me deeper into this heart forgiveness.

At the Fatherheart 'A' School I wrote a list of things that I felt I still needed to forgive my parents for. I counted the cost of what I had lost. As I did so I consciously released them from the debt that I felt they owed me. I forgave them from deep in my heart and I reached out to bless them. I began to see how wounded they had been and how unable they were to love me in the way I needed. I forgave them, especially my dad. It was a very freeing moment.

My parents were dead when I reached this point. So I did not have to test out how I reacted to them. Sometimes though, and this is true for me too, we have other people who are still alive, who we need to forgive from our heart. If we remain in a place of unforgiveness towards them it is, as Augustine said in the fourth century, like trying to make them drink poison. We pour the glass of poison which is our unforgiveness and bitterness which we push towards them hoping they will drink it. In reality we drink it ourselves and we suffer the added pain of bitterness.

On one occasion, a year or two ago, there was someone who I had sought to forgive from the heart. One day I found myself very near where they worked so I decided I would walk past to check out how it felt in my heart. I was fine as I walked past their office, so I decided to drop in to say hello. They were in and we shared a cup of coffee together and chatted. Inside of me I was testing out if I could taste poison rather than coffee. I was relieved I only tasted coffee. We parted, shook hands and I said, "God bless you" as I left. I meant it and I felt I was lighter and freer.

The session on heart forgiveness had been incredibly freeing and profound. I thought I had now dealt with my father issue. There was nothing else to do on that one until the start of the next day when James told us a long and riveting story that had happened many years before. God the Father had asked him a direct question, "James, whose son are you?" His story of this question is recounted fully in Chapter 4 of James Jordan's recently published book entitled "Sonship".

As the story unfolded, I found myself being drawn in by the Father and it was as if he was asking me the same question. "Trevor, whose son are you?"

If the question had been, "Trevor, who is your father?" I would have said John Galpin was my father. That would have been a statement of fact. In my heart however I had shut him out. As a child I had closed off my heart from him. I had explored many of those memories with Dennis and Mel and had received much healing over my responses to the pain of my childhood, the feeling of rejection, disappointment and abandonment. I had heard Jesus speak truth to me which I now knew was straight from the Father's heart. However we had never gone to that place where I had closed my heart to my father and to a lesser degree my mother. This closing off meant that I had stopped being a son in my heart to my father. I acted as a son, dutifully performing the works that I perceived a Christian should do. I remember one of the cardinal sins in my father's mind was to do with a Baptist Minister he knew who he felt had neglected his mother in her old age. I was told, "Kiss your mother, boy. You only have one mother." I had such a struggle to kiss my mother because it was put on me as a duty that I had to do. My responses as a son were all duty driven and motivated by guilt.

I would feel guilty if I did not visit them sufficiently. We struggled most times we went to see them because there was often much tension in a visit. The grandparents would kiss the children and send them off to do something quietly in another room. It was painfully familiar. "Little boys should be seen and not heard!" How I hated that attitude. We would plan a strategy to cope with visits. If events unfolded whereby we needed to make a quick exit as things began to deteriorate, as they so often did, we would execute our plan. I remember one awful visit which ended up with my father angrily demanding that we leave or he would call the police. I think there must have been some mental illness involved as his temper tantrums were so irrational. I think I may have suggested he was mentally ill on that occasion so it is no surprise he wanted to throw us out.

To some degree I had modeled this closing off of my heart to my parents to my children also. They had a great and loving open relationship with their other grandparent. Mine however they usually referred to as "Your parents." This saddens me as they never really knew my parents either.

I had closed my heart to my parents and particularly my dad, but there were others who I had looked to and considered to be like a father to me. In my early years I was actively, albeit subconsciously, looking for a father figure. One who had become a father substitute to me sexually abused me just as I entered puberty. I knew that this was one of the deep rooted causes of my subsequent turmoils which had damaged me so much in my teenage years.

I was afraid of father figures and I had a great ambivalence to any man that acted in an authoritarian and angry, paternal way to me. This explained so much why I did not trust God as a Father, because I felt that fathers were inherently dangerous. The first person that ever called me son was Dr. Criswell in Dallas, Texas, but that was just his way. I did not feel I was a son to him. Then when I met John in Florida, I met a godly father figure who I trusted and he called me son the first time I met him. I was cautious all that week but by the end I saw in him something of what a father was. As the years have gone by I have grown to love him like a father.

When this question came up on the Fatherheart School I received it as a question directed straight to me. Whose son was I? I was no-one's son, certainly not John Galpin's son. I realised that day that by doing this I had lost the heart of a son to my parents. I did not know how to be a son to them or how to be a son to God as a Father. When God said he wanted me to return to New Zealand as a son, I interpreted that as something else I had to do. I didn't know how to 'do' son. He never asked me to do son. He was talking about being a son and here I was in Kaitaia and he was explaining it to me. In closing my heart to my father and mother as a means of self protection I had deprived them of a son. This was my issue not theirs. I had just gone through an extensive time of forgiving them from my heart. I had cancelled the debt that I felt they owed me.

Now the next part that was before me was the issue of my closed heart. I had robbed my mum and dad of something very precious, an open hearted son. This was not their fault, it was mine! In the process I had also lost the heart of a son to God my Father. I had looked at God all my life like Adam did on the day of the fall in Eden and saying like Adam,

"I was afraid, I was naked, so I hid."

Revelation was sweeping over me like a waterfall. I was on the floor between the rows of chairs at the 'A' School. I was on my face before God my Father feeling wave after wave of his love sweeping over me. I was weeping and with every tear I was repenting for closing my heart, for having robbed my dad of a son. I felt if I had not been so self absorbed with my own stuff maybe I could have helped him. I could not. I could not repay him for what I had taken from him. The debt I owed my dad and my mum was too great for me to repay.

As the day unfolded we were given time to address this issue of our closed hearts. We were encouraged to write a letter to our parents or our father. Mine were both dead. They were with the Lord and healed. They already knew things that I was just now learning. So I wrote them a letter that I asked the Father to post for me! I wrote to them first to ask for their forgiveness for having closed my heart to them when I was a little boy. This letter was not about what they had or hadn't done which had led me to close my heart. It was about my behaviour and my closing of my heart to them. I wanted to ask for their forgiveness. As I wrote something very surprising began to happen. Inside of me I began to feel a huge love for them welling up that I had never felt before. I began to thank them for all the wonderful things that they had brought into my life; for the incredibly rich Christian heritage that they had given me; for having encouraged me from my earliest days to go to church and Sunday School and to read and love the Bible; for having provided us with a home, holidays, a beach hut to enjoy the summers by the sea and many other things. I thanked them that they had filled the house with older people and relatives who were full of stories, wisdom, the experiences of life and so much fun. It was flowing out of me as I was feeling the love of the Father flowing in to me. I don't know how many pivotal points you can have in your life but this was certainly one of them for me.

The rest of the week left me feeling I was walking on air. I did not know where this would lead us. We felt a heart connection with the Fatherheart Ministries team but did not know how that might develop. We drove home and looked forward to moving into our new home which was almost complete.

∾

CHAPTER NINETEEN

Growing as a Son

~

It was early 2007 that we attended our first 'A' School. We had a busy year ahead of us. We were in the final stages of completing the house that we had been building and we moved in later that month. We were very excited to have finished building the house and were enjoying the beautiful new surroundings. The business was still struggling and personally as part of the business we were completing a third edition of the glossy magazine for migrants to New Zealand that we would print and distribute in the UK in a few months time.

The business had a plan to buy the property that we were renting. It involved putting a 35% deposit down. As an investment it was a solid deal that I discussed with my accountant and our lawyer. We decided to invest in this as it would give us a part ownership of a commercial property. It involved mortgaging our new home to release the money. This was at a time when the property market was booming in New Zealand. Every business deal carries a risk and we understood this. We set the deal in motion and signed all the documents. Then left for the UK to distribute the magazine. I heard that the deal had gone through and the money transferred to the company. It all looked good.

We returned a month later and I was immediately called to the office by a rather red faced group of directors. We discovered that in our absence the money we had placed in the company for the purchase of the new building had been used to pay a number of outstanding business accounts by two of the directors. To their surprise and embarrassment between them they had used it all up. No wonder they were red faced. I discovered too that the paperwork we had signed was still sitting unsigned by the other directors. To say I was deeply concerned and disappointed by all this was a huge understatement. I felt a sense of betrayal by people I had trusted. I was to be paid interest on the loan. My lawyer was all for going after the other directors but there seemed little point because it would have caused the company to fold. More things to forgive from the heart!

Within three months I realised the company was indeed in serious financial straits. The finance director suddenly left leaving utter chaos in the accounts department. As the year began to draw to a close I knew the company could not survive and I wondered if we would survive financially too. In October one of the senior staff suddenly left and we discovered she had been planning to set up her own company. She took a number of staff with her and a group of our clients. The events of these six months were extremely stressful. Clearly some actions taken by some of the people in the company were bordering on dishonest or lacking in integrity but mostly just sheer utter incompetence.

I remember being called to a meeting with the directors in which it was suggested we spend a few days praying and fasting because Satan was attacking the company. I commented that I did not think Satan needed to attack the company as there was sufficient incompetence around the table already. Not my most charitable of comments. I had seen this for some time but was trapped on the merry go round as an investor. It was as if the whole thing was in free fall heading for collapse. I desperately wanted to pull out. I had received no income or interest payment on the loans we had made for a number of months. I calculated I had enough money left to pay my mortgage for about another eight months. It had reached crisis point. Linda and I were booked to attend the Fatherheart Ministries 'B' School in Taupo in a little over a week. I went to the office on the Wednesday and was told there was no money to pay any of the staff. They expected me to come up with some more money. I refused and I was told the company would have to shut down immediately if I did not help out. I still refused and the doors were closed a day later and the receivers were called in. In that final day I was staggered by how much equipment went missing. In a strange way I was relieved it was all over. This was not where my heart was. All of our assets were in someway tied up with this fiasco. I knew too that I was probably facing personal bankruptcy. Yet this did not really concern me. Amid all the turmoil I felt a sense of peace and that somehow God would sustain us and keep us through this financial storm. Even if I was to be bankrupted I felt I was not defined by this. I said on a number of occasions, "That is not who I am, I am not defined by this, I am a son to my heavenly Father, he will take care of us." I believed that and over the next six months I would learn to live it as we were about to lose not only the business and all of our investments, but also both our houses and cars. We were going to face total financial annihilation and that was not a happy thought!

So with all this going on we went to the 'B' School in Taupo.

We had shared a little of these recent events with James and Denise but mostly we just sat and received more of the Father's love that week. I turned my phone off for the week and did not want to speak to lawyers, accountants or creditors. The School built on the foundation of the 'A' School which we had attended in January. Many of the people on the school have since become very good friends and are now actively part of Fatherheart Ministries. One couple from Malaysia had a strong prophetic gifting in which they spoke words of life over people. James and Denise had encouraged them to come to the School to speak over all the participants.

When it came to our turn Father used them to bring some significant encouragement and direction to us. They knew nothing of our personal circumstances. The words they spoke brought life to us and hope. They spoke of us being in a confined space and that the Father was going to push the walls out in every direction. Specifically there was a strong sense that we were to go to the nations and that this would not be to one nation but many nations. They said that the truth was that the nations were waiting for us to bring the Father's love to them. The nations were calling for us. Then suddenly they paused and said that where we had been and everything that we had been doing was now in ashes. I heard an audible gasp from James and Denise. The word continued that we needed to leave it all as ashes and not try to revive anything but to step out into what the Father had for us now.

This was such a significant and accurate description of our circumstances but it had also touched the very heart of our hopes and dreams. The part about going to the nations was a confirmation of things we had known for many years. It was as if Father was saying his call had not changed on our lives. One thought occurred to me. For the last few years I had all the resources we needed to go to the nations, now we were just about to lose them all. It was as if Father was saying, "So you will just have to trust me then, son, won't you!" The next step on the journey was about to begin.

We went home after the school fortified with a very strong sense that he was with us and even though all our personal resources had just about run out, his were limitless. In the following weeks I was invited by the directors to enter a "phoenix" plan to rescue the company. This was a reference to the mythological fire bird, the phoenix rising from the ashes. I knew this was not for us and felt that Father had warned us about this while on the 'B' School. I refused to join and withdrew from all further attempts to save the company. In the new year we put both houses on the market, hoping that we would have enough left from the equity to buy a small place somewhere. That was the year that house prices tumbled in New Zealand. In the end, when we finally sold them, we were left with no equity but also no personal debt. This was a very stressful and hard time as we saw all of our assets eroding to nothing. It also became clear that company creditors were circling like vultures ready to pick the bones of the former directors. It would take another eighteen months for them to settle on me, and settle they did.

During those very testing times we made several visits to Taupo to spend time with the Fatherheart team and to talk with the Jordans. One weekend there had been a teaching shared about Father raising up a Caleb generation. Caleb was eighty years old when he asked God to give him his mountain of his inheritance. We were in our mid fifties and were wondering what the plan was now that all our resources had gone. During that weekend I had a strong sense that we were to move to Taupo and join the ministry there. I had no idea what that would look like but I did know that they needed a gardener at the Eden Centre. Linda had been working for five years at a Hospice in Tauranga and we had always looked at her job as a back up in times when we needed extra income. We knew there was a Hospice in Taupo too. Then that weekend she distinctly heard the Father say to her that he no longer wanted her to work with the dying but the living. We began to talk with James and Denise about these things. They were tremendously encouraging and supportive. However we had no idea what we would do if we joined Fatherheart Ministries as it was a faith based Ministry where everyone is responsible for their own financial support and income. We had neither financial support nor income! Neither of us would have jobs in Taupo. Yet we had a growing sense that Father was leading us in this. I had no real desire to speak or preach I just wanted to be part of this family who shared the same Father.

I heard that James was going to visit Australia and speak at a number of conferences. I asked if I could go with him to drive or carry his bag or something. It was agreed and Linda would come over and join us for the last week in Sydney. During those three weeks we had an offer made on our house and after some painful negotiations we agreed a price that meant both houses were sold but we would have nothing left at the end. Mid way through the trip James spoke on the Father of compassion and the God of all comfort from 2 Corinthians chapter 1 verse 4.

Praise be to the God and Father of our Lord Jesus Christ, the Father of compassion and the God of all comfort, who comforts us in all our troubles, so that we can comfort those in any trouble with the comfort we ourselves have received from God.

This touched me deeply because this was what I desperately needed.

During a ministry time James talked about how the Father uses us to represent him by being his arms. He shared how Jack Winter believed that the revelation of the Father's love could be imparted through this embrace. At the end of the talk James asked if anyone would like to receive a human embrace to represent the Father's arms and to receive Father's comforting love through this. I knew this was what I needed. I had somehow managed to avoid this until then. This time I ran to receive the Father's embrace. All my own efforts and resources had left me naked and stressed and here was the Father extending his compassionate loving arms to hold me. I had vowed twelve years earlier that I would not depend on anyone for my finances. I would do it myself. It was so orphan like.

Now here I was, I had nothing left and Father was saying, "Let's go to the nations but in my strength and in my way."

That day he came to me as a loving Father. As I was held by someone who represented the Father's arms, God the Father himself poured so much comfort and love into me. The person had a rather wet shoulder at the end!

A couple of days later half way through the conference, in one of the coffee breaks, James came to me and asked me if I would like to share something in the next session. This was about to start in less than ten minutes. My mind went straight into overload. What should I share? What topic? What verse? How long? The answers I got were not what I was expecting.

James said, "Share something that is in your heart, something of your story, of the journey Father has you on, for about fifteen minutes and don't mention the Bible!"

I was stunned. I always spoke from the Bible and usually a verse or two and what's more I do not talk about myself! All of my training reacted to this. Anyway I shared and I talked about me! If you have read this far you will know that I have now learnt to do this. On that day it was a huge challenge. James was not saying don't prepare or don't quote the Bible but he knew that I needed to learn to speak from my heart. The journey the Father had me on was my journey. He knew that people would connect at heart level as we shared what Father had done in our hearts. He knew that I could do the teaching from the Word but he was encouraging me to speak from my heart.

A week later he asked me again. Same thing but this time to take half an hour!

The Father was about to have us embark with him on a journey that is all about growing daily as sons and trusting him each step of the way to provide for us and meet our everyday needs. We had lived like that before many years ago when we were missionaries in Italy, but we were very out of practice. It felt like going to the gym after not having done any exercise for a very long time. Our spiritual muscles in this area of walking by faith and trusting him for finances were very under used and were going to ache for quite some time to come.

We shared with James and Denise about what we felt Father was saying about joining the team. They suggested some areas that they felt we could help in, one of which was developing a network or family of people who were connected at heart with Fatherheart Ministries. This was already in place to some degree but they felt it needed revamping. We agreed that we would look at this and see what Father had in mind. This would involve a trip to Europe to attend a Fatherheart gathering in The Netherlands to meet many of the key people in Europe who related to the Ministry. We both felt we should go. In our dwindling resources we had enough money for two return tickets. If we used this it would empty the bank account. We sensed that Father was saying to go and he would look after all our needs. So we booked the flights.

The house sale went through and we moved all of our furniture and personal possessions into storage to Taupo. It was a hard wrench leaving our lovely beach home and stepping into the unknown but we had a great sense of Father leading us through. One of the things that had come back to our minds in those days of moving from Tauranga to Taupo was the prophetic picture that had been given to us five years before. It was of an extinct volcano and that the first place we would go to would be an extinct volcano but the second place would be by an active volcano. The first place would not be where we would flourish in the sense of ministry, but the second would be a place of great release in terms of ministry. We had always interpreted this is a spiritual sense and had thought it was all about the first church we had gone to. The church situation had been like an extinct volcano and when we moved on into new things we presumed this might be the active part. Now, however we were physically moving from Tauranga where at the mouth of the harbour sits Mt Maunganui, an extinct volcano. Taupo, where we were moving to is on the shore of Lake Taupo, at the end of the lake is Mt Ruapehue a very active volcano. In fact all around Taupo there is geothermal activity. We suddenly saw that this word may after all have been geographical rather than spiritual. This gave us added hope and encouragement.

We flew to Europe as planned with James and Denise a few weeks later. The visit was very successful in that we got to meet with most of our family and friends in the UK and made many new friends in the wider Fatherheart Ministries family. We also visited Malaysia and met again with the couple who had brought words of life to us at the 'B' School. On returning to New Zealand we went straight to the first of the Inheriting the Nations, three month long schools that FHM was conducting on Great Barrier Island off the coast of New Zealand. I was booked to teach a two week course on Church History at the School.

On the last day of our two weeks of teaching the whole school gathered to pray for us as we were very much launching out into the unknown after we left. There was a clear call on us to go to the nations and we were beginning to make new connections with various Fatherheart people but it was not clear to us how that would unfold. We had all of our furniture in temporary storage but no idea where we would live or how we would fund ourselves once we returned to Taupo. As the school began to pray for us one of the students came and gave us a Chinese bank note which was worth about $2. She said it was the first fruit of an offering. James took this theme up and said he felt that Father was asking them to take up a love offering for us as we stepped out with him on this journey. My reaction on hearing this was to feel inside that I did not deserve this. This was a typical orphan like response. Linda saw my reaction and suggested that maybe Father wanted to bring some healing to me on this. They decided to hold the offering on the Sunday, the day after we had left Orama.

That evening I was sitting in the class room thinking through this issue of not feeling I deserved the Father's provision. I remembered the vow I had made thirteen years before that I would never let myself be dependent on Christians again for my income. I would manage my own finances. Well, we had done that for all those years and whilst we had done well initially here we were left with nothing and facing bankruptcy at some point. Now we had met God as a Father and he was asking us to join him on this journey and he had said that he would provide and meet our needs.

My reaction had been, "Well I'll see how we get on for a year and then review it."

I still had a lot of learning to do in this area of trusting the Father to provide for us in our finances. I was still calling them 'our finances'. My whole mind set was orphan like in this area. As I was sitting thinking about this, one of the students came in and sat down. Jane began to tell me what she had just seen. She had been in the small shop that they had at Orama when the two young teenage children of one of the couples on the school came in. Their dad was in the shop too. The younger of the two went up to her father and asked if she could have some money to buy some sweets. Apparently he opened his wallet and said, "Take whatever you want!"

Then Jane said to me, "That is so like Father, not what we need but what we want!" Then she danced off somewhere.

I sat there with my mouth open. Indeed that was so like Father. I was worrying about what we needed, but he was interested in the desires of our hearts. I felt him say he would more than take care of our needs and that it would be good to think about our desires too as he wanted to bless us more than we could imagine, simply because he loves us. At that point I was not sure what my desires were but I had a good idea what we needed.

We left and went to Taupo. On Sunday evening I had a phone call from Denise. She asked me to sit down because she had news for me. She said that they had taken up the love offering for us that evening and she wanted to tell us what it was. She paused and then said it was $37,000 New Zealand dollars. I was flabbergasted. Here was the first of what was to be many expressions of Father's provision. This was more than sufficient to enable us to find a house to rent in Taupo, pay the deposit and live while we began to organise the next stage of the journey. We were elated, encouraged, humbled and just really chuffed! This truly felt like a brand new day. This money was placed in the Fatherheart account in Taupo and used to pay for various ministry related expenses.

Nine months later we were in Malaysia with James and Denise teaching on an 'A' School. I was sharing about the Orphan Spirit. I was describing the attitude and behaviour typical of living like orphans. As I was teaching, back in New Zealand exactly at that moment, in a court I was being declared a bankrupt. I knew this was happening but I really knew in my heart that I was not defined by this. I am a son with a very wealthy Father who not only meets our every need but who also gives us the desires of our hearts.

As I write these words I am sitting over looking a beautiful sandy beach in Zanzibar. It is a weekend rest before we start another 'A' School in a few days time on the mainland in Tanzania. We have discovered that Father is very interested in us resting and enjoying his world. Also as I write my name is being removed from the list of bankrupts in New Zealand. I am discharged. We have paid all outstanding debts, we owe nothing.

∼

CHAPTER TWENTY

Welcome Home

~

We have felt so welcomed and loved by the team that makes up Fatherheart Ministries. After many years on the journey we have finally felt we have come home. They know the story and the twists and turns of the road that we have walked. We feel accepted and we do not feel judged. Instead we feel greatly loved and included.

Within this ministry we often meet people who have had experiences and have faced challenges similar to our own. Many feel they have fallen from grace and have been excluded and rejected. Others feel they have been disconnected in someway from both the church and even God. One of the visions that we share is to see these people brought back into their place within the family of God and to discover that God is their real Father.

The Christian world is sadly regularly rocked by reports of high profile Christians who fail in some way and are disgraced as a result. The word disgraced sums it up, they are viewed as 'dis - graced'. This is much more widespread in the church than just a few big name failures. Most of us know pastors and church leaders who fall and whose lives and the lives of their families and churches are devastated as a result. It is a widespread and tragic phenomenon.

There are also members of the church who succumb to sin and failure. Much of this the church grades with degrees of seriousness often based on a somewhat arbitrary system. For example whilst the Bible says that God hates pride this does not figure in most church lists of unacceptable sin. Sexual sins rank very highly as would be expected but these are then categorized into levels of seriousness. As cultures have changed over the years some sexual sins seem to have moved down the scale and others up. Pre marital sex is dealt with less severely nowadays, though extra marital sex has always been close to the top. Some consider same sex sexual activity as more serious than anything else.

The Bible however does not grade sin. Sin is sin and needs to be repented of. How people who have fallen into sin are handled varies widely and many opinions are proffered about what should be done. Many of them and their families become casualties as the church often puts the fallen leaders out for target practice. The church sadly has a long history of slaughtering its own wounded.

Then there are people who are disciplined by churches for other issues such as rebelliousness, for holding heretical beliefs, lack of submission to leadership and so on. These vary from church to church and denomination to denomination. Many people feel ejected from Church and rejected by other Christians for a host of different reasons. They have given offence and many take offence. Whilst they still have their faith in God, they have lost faith in the church and are lost in the sense of no longer being part of a church. These people often feel they have been wrenched out of a local church through hurt and disruptions, becoming victims of people's agendas, control and manipulation. They have lost their place of belonging and connection. Many fall foul of a system that is built on the leaders and frail leaders at that. When leaders fall into sin the church and its people can become some of the casualties who are caught in the fall out.

As I reflect on these issues it seems there is a process of what happens to Christians and particularly Christian leaders who fall into serious sin, or have a 'fall from grace'. I believe there is a biblical response that demonstrates the love of the Father for them and their families, a healing of their hearts and a complete restoration. This is what I mean by being brought back "into grace". The revelation of the Father's love is a vital key to restoring those who have lost their place in the Church of God.

In Luke Chapter 15 there is a Biblical perspective on these issues, which gives a model to guide and help us in this process of seeing people restored to fellowship and to help them reconnect with the body of Christ. In this passage there are three parables that Jesus tells. The parables of the lost sheep, the lost coin and the prodigal son. This last parable has been used by many to teach truth about the Father's love for us. I would rather call it the parable of the lost sons because the older brother is as lost as the younger one.

The basic meaning of these parables is the same. It is simply that there is great joy in heaven over one lost person who is reunited in his relationship with God. Classically these stories have been used by many evangelists. Also every Fatherheart teacher has taught with great effectiveness on the story of the Prodigal. It has become a popular passage for those wanting to reveal the heart of God the Father since Jesus has his Father in mind as he speaks.

In chapter 1 of his gospel Luke says he has put together an "orderly account". Matthew is the only other gospel writer who records the story of the lost sheep. It is only Luke who records the two additional stories of the lost coin and the lost sons. It raises the question, has the Holy Spirit got a specific reason to bring this material together in such a way? I believe he does. Luke had learnt to write what the Father, through the Holy Spirit, told him.

According to these stories a sheep, a coin and possibly two sons are "lost". Whilst these parables have been seen traditionally as evangelistic there is however another aspect to them. The common feature here is that all three stories describe situations where what is lost was originally not lost. The sheep was once one of one hundred in the flock, not a goat. The coin was one of ten on the dowry chain not a random coin. The son was a son not a run away slave. There is more in the parables than we first think.

The common denominator was that they had all been in relationship and for a variety of reasons became fragmented or removed from their place where they once belonged. The language I am using is not about whether they are "saved" but about being out of relationship. All were essentially lost but to see this as lost in the traditional sense may be to miss something that the Father wants us to see.

In the first parable there is a lost sheep. There are forty-million sheep in New Zealand so I know a little about them. We even had a small flock that we shared with a neighbour once. Their main activity is to eat grass! They move from tuft of grass to tuft of grass. They are very focused, but stupid. Step by step, mouthful by mouthful they wander away from the rest of the flock, their eyes on the immediate and on the next mouthful. Consequently they end up not where they should be but far away from the rest of the flock.

This can be so like people who have just lost their way through constant activity. They are feeding on the latest programme promoted by churches with the best intentions, but very busy and so often performance driven. They can become casualties of the good intentions of task focused leadership and churches. A purpose driven church may be helpful but such intensive programmes have left a whole generation exhausted and disillusioned. They feel that they were just faithfully getting on with serving God, and wonder to themselves, how did they end up exhausted and burnt out? They are good people who are lost and alone and may be desperately out of touch with the church and the Father's love.

The coin was probably one of ten on a dowry chain which for some reason is disconnected and lost in a dark corner of a first century Jewish house. It lays in the dark, forcefully torn from its rightful place in the relationship previously enjoyed. It is helpless, it can't do anything to get back where it came from. I am putting human characteristics on to a coin, but many people are like this coin torn out of church life not by their own actions but by the actions of others and sometimes by leaders with agendas. When we were missionaries in Italy we were ejected from our Missionary society over the issue of the baptism of the Holy Spirit so understand something of such a trauma and the powerlessness of situations

In the third parable the younger son deliberately makes the choice to leave the family. He is "lost" because what was buried in his heart came to the surface and he began to live it out. Many Christians tragically fall into this type of behaviour. There is a progressive nature to the son's fall. At some point he crossed a line. Perhaps it was it when he asked for his share of the inheritance. In one sense he was asserting his independence. For a while he stayed at home yet it seems he is planning his leaving. Has he sinned in his heart already, did he plan what he was going to do? It is like the words of the Lord to Cain in Genesis 4 verse 7

"..sin is crouching at your door; it desires to have you, but you must master it."

Many of us recognise this tension. When the son got to the new place in the far country, what he had planned and decided to do in his heart he put into practice. Very seldom do Christians who fall do it spontaneously. The reality is they have toyed with sin in their hearts already. The activity is just an expression of what had been stirring in their hearts for some time. The devil's tactics are that he tempts us which builds up the internal pressure. Then he describes the pleasures of sin which lead us to try to justify the activity. Next he minimizes the seriousness and calls us to cover it up. Most sins committed by Christians are rooted in unhealed issues of the heart.

It is interesting that we are not told of the exact nature of the son's sinful behavior. We don't know if it was gambling, drinking or drugs or buying sex from women or boys, or overeating and gluttony. Perhaps he spent it all on chocolate, or buying friends, or buying a big house and filling it with wild parties. All we know is, it cost him everything and it was wild. The older brother does not know what his brother spent his money on either but makes a judgment based on ignorance and possibly his own weakness.

It is only when the younger son begins to feel the pain of his circumstances and the associated shame that he comes to his senses and wants to change. As long as he is enjoying his sinful lifestyle he is not going to change. When the cash runs out and the reality begins to bite then he begins to change his heart. At this stage he is not repentant but he is uncomfortable. He gets a job, which is a sensible thing to do when he runs out of money. It is only when the pain of his circumstances becomes overwhelming that he begins to see the reality of the situation. The younger son in the story is becoming repentant.

This process is what happens when Christians fall into sin. Much of it is hidden. The fact that often someone is caught out by their sinful behavior doesn't mean they are necessarily repentant. Repentance is born in the heart not as a result of being caught. Being caught results in shame rather than repentance. This is a crucial issue when ministering to the fallen. Where they are in this process is important. This is one of issues that Danny Silk raised in his book which I have already referred to chapter thirteen.

The older brother is in a very different situation. He hasn't left the home. He hasn't obviously sinned like the younger brother but in his heart he has lost so much. It is all below the surface and internal rather than obvious misbehaviour. However the true state of his heart begins to emerge when the younger brother returns home and this challenges his world. His reaction is described in verse 28.

He is full of anger and refuses to go into the party that his father has thrown for the homecoming brother. The older brother stays outside burning with resentment and sulking. When the father goes out to him the boy's hidden attitudes all surface. His attitude to his father was that he had slaved for him. These are not the words of a willing and loving son but the words of a servant-hearted labourer. He has just been giving him grudging obedience. Generally obedience is a response when a person does not want to do something or has to do it out of duty or fear or as an order from a superior. The son's use of this language betrays an underlying attitude of broken relationship.

The older son could not call his brother by name or relationship, he simply refers to him when addressing his father as 'this son of yours'. He does not want to own him as his brother. Added to that he judgmentally jumps to conclusions by assuming the younger brother has spent all his money on prostitutes. He has not met his brother yet so this is pure speculation. Having said that it may indicate what is happening in his secret life. It is not as if prostitutes are only found in a 'far country'. They can be found in every community. Rather like the Pharisees, who were listening to Jesus tell this story, they knew who the prostitutes were in their towns. When one came into Simon the Pharisee's house to anoint Jesus feet, Simon knew exactly who she was and she had not been denied entry to the house. Jesus after all did not call the Pharisees whited sepulchers for nothing.

It may not have been a happy ending for this boy as we are left not knowing whether he went into the party or not.

The tragedy of so much over the centuries is that the 'older brother attitude' has sadly dominated the church and how it treats people. When the goats get saved they make them behave like sheep and the older brothers run courses on how to toe the line and eat grass. The older brothers can so easily, without realizing it get caught up with rejecting and ejecting, disciplining and ruling, getting people in line. They hate freedom and feasting. They know how to get rid of the nonconformists. They are so often theological perfectionists. They specialize in making judgments and when it comes to the fallen they form the firing squads. They become the judge and jury and they have long memories.

Those who carried the 'older brother attitude' staffed the Church Councils and the Inquisition. They condemned Jan Huss and then the Lutherans. They opposed every new move of God. They presided over the burnings of the Anabaptists and of witches. They hounded out the Methodist preachers from the churches. They condemned Wilberforce as an enthusiast. They ridiculed the Pentecostals and declared the move of God in Toronto as demonic. They say that Fatherheart teachers have abandoned Jesus.

All the four main characters of these parables, the sheep, the coin, and both sons are lost and the Christian world today is full of people like this.

There is a point in each story where a change occurs and something happens. In the case of the lost sheep it continues on its own solitary journey, just drifting off, head down, hardly noticing it is lost. It is consumed with an endless cycle of activity. It could end up outside away from the flock like this for ever, therefore the shepherd goes seeking for the sheep. This is the proactive part of the ministry of the shepherd.

The coin is unable to get itself back. People that have been torn out of church and rejected are hardly likely to find their own way back unless someone reaches out to them. It needs the church led by the Holy Spirit to be proactive in seeking them.

There is a much more detailed account of the thought processes of the younger son as he thinks about returning home. When his pain was greater than his shame he began to come to his senses. This is crucial in restoring fallen leaders and Christians caught in sin. The place of coming to their senses is different in every situation and not much can be done until there is a desire to return on their part. The younger son had a moment of coming to his senses. He made the first move and as soon as the father saw this he ran to the son.

In all three stories we see God being proactive in seeking out the lost. One of the main points of these stories is the common thread that runs through them; there is great joy in heaven when the lost come home. In these stories the intensity of the joy increases. For the sheep it is one out of a hundred. For the coins it is one out of ten. In the story of the lost sons there is joy when the younger son returns. So much so that the father longs for the older son to participate in party also. All of the Godhead are involved in the process of restoring the lost and the fallen back into the family. All three persons of the Trinity are actively participating in the restoration of the lost.

The shepherd in the first story without doubt is a picture of Jesus. In the Old Testament we read of the Shepherd of Israel and this imagery would not have been lost on the Pharisees. David's description of the Lord in Psalm 23 is of a shepherd. Jesus describes himself in John chapter 10 as the Good Shepherd who lays down his life for the sheep. In this story the Shepherd actively seeks the lost sheep. Jesus says after he leaves Zacchaeus' house, in Luke chapter 19 verse 10, that the Son of Man came to seek and save the lost. So often sheep run from the shepherd, they are not all fluffy little lambs, they have dags and mess, dirt and filth. Nevertheless he carries them on his shoulders. It is a very practical solution.

In the second parable of the lost coin, many have seen the housewife with the lamp in her hand as the church, with the Holy Spirit represented by a lamp. The Bible describes the Holy Spirit as a light to the nations and a lamp to our feet. The light of the Holy Spirit shines into the dark places. In some places in the Bible, the Church is depicted as the bride of Christ. If this was a dowry chain worn by a bride it would be her most precious possession. Without the light the woman would not have been able to find the coin. The Church as the bride needs the light of the Spirit to seek out the rejected and abandoned, who have become lost from the church.

The last story without a doubt is a picture of the Father himself. The father in the story wonderfully illustrates the way God our Father treats those who are separated in some way from him. Also how he welcomes home Christians who have fallen in sin and the older brothers in the church who have no sense of sonship or intimacy with him as Father.

Luke chapter 15 verse 20 describes the father in the story as watching constantly for his son. This is before he is on the horizon, watching every day perhaps, waiting and longing for the son to return. When the father sees him coming, he identifies him from a distance, recognizes him immediately and is filled with compassion. He is moved with pity and tenderness. We know that Jesus has his Father in mind as he speaks these words. In Exodus chapter 34 the Lord describes himself as a compassionate God full of love and forgiveness when he reveals his glory to Moses. Paul, in 2 Corinthians chapter 1 verse 4 describes him as the Father of compassion and the God of all comfort. In this story Jesus says the father has compassion on his son and runs to him. This is a powerful combination of emotions and actions and this is all before he has heard anything from his son. He makes no judgment about the boy. Instead the father runs to the son. He wants to get to him before the son changes his mind or turns away perhaps uncertain and fearful of how he will be received. This is the most difficult moment for returning fallen or broken people. How will they be received? How will people react? Will they be welcome? The father wants to get to the returning son before anyone else does. If the older brother had got to him first it would have been a different story.

When the father reaches the boy he embraces him. He throws

his arms around him in an active passionate embrace of acceptance and love. Then Jesus says the father kisses him fervently. This is total unconditional acceptance. There are echoes of Eden here. When God created Adam in Genesis chapter 2 he breathed into Adam's nostrils the breathe of life which would have looked very much like a kiss.

All of this takes place before the son says a thing. He has not made his speech yet. The son begins his preplanned, much rehearsed speech and doesn't get very far before the father interrupts him. The father then continues his restoration of the son. The primary issue in having a heart for a fallen individual is acceptance and restoration. The restoration of the wounded and broken heart is essential in the process and includes issues of repentance and healing of the heart.

This is only a story but all the fallen need this acceptance and unconditional love. When they return they need acceptance not rejection, they need love and mercy not judgement. They are anxious and afraid and they will need reassurance by their family and friends. They do not need the harsh attitudes and judgement of the older brother. Paul, when he addresses this issue, in Galatians chapter 6 verse 1 talks about restoring the fallen gently.

"Brothers, if someone is caught in a sin, you who are spiritual should restore him gently."

They also need help straight away. There is an urgency in Jesus' story. "Quick" says the father in verse 22. When the fallen come home there is a need for urgency in embracing them and beginning to work with them. It can't be left, there is an acute need for them, and particularly their family, to receive support and help with trusted friends gathering around them.

Then the father calls for the servants to bring the best robe. I have often wondered who would have owned the best robe. I believe it would have been the father's own cloak. This cloak would have wrapped the son in the father's very own clothes. He did not want anyone to see him in this state. The robe covers the dirt and dust from the journey and the stink of the pig pen. No one would be able to look on him and see his shameful appearance. The shame in his heart would have been huge. He would have keenly felt his failure, his stupid self indulgence. He would have felt a disappointment, that he had let everyone down and he would have been afraid to have looked anyone in the eye. The older brother may well have tried to expose him, reject him, or turn him away. However the father has one clear objective. The father covers his son's shame with his own cloak. The issue of shame is huge and well documented. Any ministry that seeks to share the love of the Father needs to understand the issues of shame. There is hope and there is no need to hide. God our real Father covers our nakedness and shame with is unconditional love.

Next in the story the father calls for the ring. When the son had left home for the far country he would have been wearing a ring that spoke of his position as a son. It was a ring of authority. When he was in the far country he lost the ring, maybe he even sold it for food. When he returns the father calls for the servants to bring the ring. The servants who received this instruction did not stop to question which ring. The father must have had another ring prepared awaiting the return. It is as if the father had absolutely refused to give up on the lost son. How like God our Father who has prepared a way for the lost to come home. The father calls for the ring and reinstates the relationship between them. Even though the boy had squandered his inheritance he is now welcomed home again as a son. This is not what the son was expecting. He did not feel worthy of being a son. However the father in the story ignores this. He calls for the ring of sonship to be placed on his finger.

The father then calls for the shoes. Only free men or sons would have worn shoes. Slaves and servants wore no shoes. This is a powerful visual reminder to all who saw him that not only was he welcome home but he was also reinstated in his position as a son within the family. It is a statement that he is the son of the family not the slave or servant. For those who have fallen from a place of ministry there is a great need to bring the matter to a conclusion. This does not necessarily mean a reinstatement to a specific ministry role but a willingness to release the individual to a place of acceptance. This marks the end of the process. This is a sign to the world that restoration has taken place. In some cases it may be a restoration to a ministry role but this is not essential. More important than restoration to ministry is the restoration of the heart of a son to the Father. Many have sought to reestablish ministry and neglected the heart only to fall again. Ministry and performance are issues so often of orphan-hearted behaviour rather than sonship.

Suitably dressed, the son is welcomed back into the house as the father throws a party to celebrate. The celebration of his return marks the end of the process. There needs to be an end. Exile and banishment serve no purpose. When the fallen are released and restoration has taken place then a public recognition of that fact needs to be made. A public end to the process makes it clear to all that restoration has happened. So often when people fall there is great sadness and many are caught up in the fall out and are wounded and hurt. They too need to see a clear ending to the process for themselves and the sake of the one they love. However not all are restored and welcomed back. Sadly the attitude of the older brother can prevail even when someone has been restored.

When the older brother protests and judges his brother he refuses to join in the celebration. Then the father goes out to him pleading with him to come in and join the party. The father in the parable loves the older brother as much as the younger. The father's response to the older son is to go out to him and plead with him to come to the party. The father is acting as an advocate for the younger son in verses 31 and 32.

> *"'My son,' the father said, 'you are always with me, and everything I have is yours. But we had to celebrate and be glad, because this brother of yours was dead and is alive again; he was lost and is found.' '*

The son cannot speak for himself. He needs someone to speak for him.

There is a great need for advocates in these circumstances especially in the face of the older brother's attitude. The fallen cannot speak for themselves and need others to speak for them. An advocate knows the heart of the fallen, knows if their repentance is genuine and real. They know when they are ready for restoration and release. Without this key role in place it is very difficult for the fallen to ever be fully restored in their relationships with those who may have been damaged by their actions.

To those who bring a revelation of the Father's love it includes a clear mandate from the Father to welcome home the fallen and seek to restore them to functioning healthy members of the family of God. In this there is great joy. Celebration and joy are the themes that run through the conclusion of each of these parables as they reflect the heart of the Father.

~

CHAPTER TWENTY ONE

Celebrating Weakness

~

For the last three years we have been literally on a journey with our Father. We travel for most of the year visiting people who are connected in some way with Fatherheart Ministries and teaching at Fatherheart Schools and conferences. This takes us to places as far apart as Finland and Uganda, Northern Ireland and Virginia, ministering and teaching on the revelation of the Father's love.

Everywhere we go we meet people on the same journey as us, discovering the depths of the Father's love for them.

We have found huge fulfillment and joy on this journey. I do not think we work any the less hard than we have done in the past but there is greater joy on this journey because we are doing it from a place of enjoying the Father's presence and resting in his arms and in his love for us. We do not do this out of a sense of duty or of having to, instead we are following him wherever he goes. In the past I was eager to serve him and be obedient. I still am, but I am coming from a totally different place now. I serve him as a son who delights to accompany his Father wherever he is at work. I do not do it out of duty but out joy and anticipation. I had not realised that the Christian life could be so enjoyable. Many times when people ask us how we cope with the traveling, they have a look on their faces that is often of earnest concern. It is as if they are expecting us to say,

"Oh, you know, we are suffering for the sake of the gospel" or something like that. Instead my answer tends to surprise them because I say, "We love it! It is what we have been made for."

C.S.Lewis once said that the serious business of heaven is joy. I am discovering this to be true. We are so enjoying our Christian walk. In 1 John chapter 2 verses 5 and 6 the apostle writes,

> *"This is how we know we are in him: Whoever claims to live in him must walk as Jesus did".*

This begs the question, how did Jesus walk? A few years ago people used to wear bracelets with the letters WWJD on them which stood for What Would Jesus Do? I am not sure what people made of that question. I guess if you had asked me a few years ago I would have given a list of things we had to do to be like Jesus, most of which I had not had great success in doing. So the bracelets were often discarded as yet another good idea that did not work.

We used to think that we are supposed to walk with Jesus. We are not asked to do that in the Bible since we are in Christ. Instead we walk as he walked. So how did Jesus walk? He walked daily in relationship with his Father, enjoying his love and approval. Doing the things he saw his Father doing and saying the things he heard his Father saying and only those things. John chapter 5 verses 19 and 20 are clear examples of this. Jesus said,

*"I tell you the truth, the Son can do nothing by himself; he
can do only what he sees his Father doing, because whatever
the Father does the Son also does. For the Father loves the
Son and shows him all he does".*

This filled Jesus' life with joy as he walked like this. So walking
as he walked is all about living out of that place of being in the
Father's love.

On numerous occasions Jesus was filled with incredible joy and
talked about the pleasure that he experienced with the Father.
In Matthew 11 verses 25 - 30 and in the parallel passage in Luke
Chapter 10 verse 21, Jesus is praying or rather praising his Father
and Luke says he is filled with joy by the Holy Spirit. Luke's word
literally means to jump for joy! I have this mental picture of Jesus
jumping for joy and punching the air with a shout of "Yes!" He says
to the Father

*"I thank you Father that you have hidden these things from
the wise and learned and revealed them to little children.
Yes, Father, for this was your good pleasure."*

He is talking about the things that that the Father has shown
him. He continues,

*"No one knows the Son except the Father and no one knows
the Father except the Son and those to whom the Son chooses
to reveal him."*

There is such a sense of mutual delight between them. Jesus walked in joyful union and communion with the Father and his desire is to share that with us. In the very next verse in Matthew 11 Jesus expands on how we walk in him and how this works for us. He then says,

"Come to me all you who are weary and burdened and I will give you rest".

That is so comforting and reassuring. He then says,

"Take my yoke upon you and learn from me, for I am gentle and humble in heart and you will find rest for your souls. For my yoke is easy and my burden is light".

For years as I read this it mystified me how this was meant to help us rest when it seems to suggest that here is yet more that we have to do. From my place of being a servant hearted orphan I only saw this as something extra to carry which I did not do very well. I could not see how carrying a yoke was going to be easy or light.

Recently we were speaking at a pastor's conference in Addis Ababa, Ethiopia and I was talking with some of the pastors there who were also farmers. In talking about these verses I received a better understanding as they told me how ploughing a field with a team of oxen worked. If the farmer had a team of four oxen or even just two the leading couple of oxen were made up of an experienced older ox on one side who carried the whole weight of the yoke on its shoulders. Teamed beside it under the same yoke was a younger inexperienced ox who was being trained to pull the plough. This ox could barely feel the weight of the yoke as the older one carried it all. Suddenly I saw the picture. Jesus walked with his Father who carried the weight of the yoke on his shoulders and Jesus the Son was yoked there with him. So when Jesus tells us to take his yoke because it is easy and light he is saying to walk as he walks is to be under the shadow of the Father, who carries the weight of the yoke. No wonder he jumps for joy! To walk as Jesus walked is walking in total dependence on the Father, rejoicing in his provision and protection.

When my son was a little boy he had a plastic car that he could push along the path. The children called it Beep Beep. One day when I was cutting the grass at our house I was walking down the lawn, making sure my lines were straight when I became aware that someone was following me. At the end of the grass I stopped and there he was pushing Beep Beep along. I asked him what he was doing. He replied that he was cutting the grass. I encouraged him to continue and to keep his eye on my back so he did not get any wiggles in the lines. We paced up and down the lawn together. When I had finished he turned to me and said, "I've cut the grass Dad." "Well done son, that was a great job." I replied. He scampered off to tell his mother that he had cut the grass. This is a picture of how we walk as Jesus walked, in step with the Fatherfollowing him and keeping our eye on his back. His yoke is easy and his burden is light.

In Luke chapter 12 verse 32, Jesus says,

"Do not be afraid, little flock, for your Father has been pleased to give you the kingdom."

Again Jesus shares the pleasure the Father takes in us when he gives us the kingdom. The Kingdom is that place where the Father's love is being poured out and made manifest. It delights him to share this with their sons and daughters who make up the little flock. I am increasingly discovering the joy that is in the Father's heart when we know his love. In the final prayer that Jesus prayed before he left the upper room and went out to the garden of Gethsemane he prayed that his disciples might have the full measure of his joy within them (John 17 verse 13). Jesus' expectation was that our Christian lives would also reflect the incredible amount of joy that he experienced each day walking with his Father. This is part of our inheritance as the sons and daughters of Almighty God, to be filled with the same measure of joy that Father, Son and Spirit share together.

So we are beginning to really enjoy our Christian lives. We enjoyed some things before but for me it was such hard work trying to please God all the time. Always struggling to get his approval. Now I know he really loves me as my real Father. He was there to catch me when I fell and hold me in his arms of love. We are learning now to rest in him, enjoy being a son and a daughter.

It is not as if there are no struggles and challenges but the joy that we are discovering in this journey of walking and living in the love of the Father is amazing. We are learning that we do not have to be strong and have all the answers. We are learning to rejoice in our weaknesses since it makes us more dependent on our Father. He takes the yoke and we get to join in all the fun. What better way of living can there be?

≈

RESOURCES AND RECOMMENDED READING

Fatherheart Ministries - www.fatherheart.net
James and Denise Jordan's ministry website. Including resources, team itineraries and information about Fatherheart Ministries week long A and B Schools. Complete with online store.

Trevor and Linda Galpin's - www.trevorlindafhm.com
This website includes Trevor's blog, resources, itinerary and ways of supporting them.

A Father to You - www.afathertoyou.com
Mark Gyde's website with lots of audio and video teachings, teaching materials and inspirational videos.

Fatherheart TV - www.fatherheart.tv
Inspirational videos and weekly live webcasts to inspire and help you grow in the love of the Father.

Jesus and his Father – by his family and friends
Trevor's latest book available from Amazon.com *&* www.fatherheart.net

BOOKS

Sonship - By James Jordan

A Father to you - By Mark Gyde

The Shack Revisited - By C. Baxter Krueger

AN INVITATION...

If you enjoyed reading this book we invite you to a Fatherheart Ministries 'A' School. Fatherheart Ministries 'A' Schools are a one week environment of the revelation of love.

The Two Goals of 'A' Schools are:

1. To give an opportunity for you to have a personal major experience of the love that God the Father has for you.

2. To give the strongest Biblical understanding possible of the place of the Father in the Christian life and walk.

During the school you will be introduced to the full perspective of the revelation of Father's love. Through revelatory insight and sound biblical teaching told through the lives of those that minister you will be exposed to a transforming message of Love, Life and Hope.

You will be given the opportunity to remove the main blockages to receiving Father's love and discover your heart as a true son or daughter. Jesus had the heart of a son to His Father. He lived in the presence of the love of the Father. John's Gospel tells us that everything that He said and did was what He saw and heard His Father doing. Jesus invites us to enter that world as brothers and sisters of Him the first born.

As we open our hearts Father pours His love into our hearts by the Holy Spirit. In a heart transformed by His love, true and lasting change will occur. After years of striving and perfomance many are finally finding the way home, to a place of rest and belonging.

To apply for an A School visit 'Schools & Events' at

www.fatherheart.net

Additional copies of this book and other resources
from Fatherheart Media are available at:

www.fatherheart.net/shop - New Zealand
www.fatherheartmedia.com - Europe
www.amazon.com - Paperback & Kindle versions

FATHERHEART MEDIA

PO BOX 1039
Taupo, 3330, New Zealand

Visit us at www.fatherheart.net

Printed in Poland
by Amazon Fulfillment
Poland Sp. z o.o., Wrocław